Business Faces the Urban Crisis

john s. morgan

consultant
employee relations communication
general electric company
new york, new york

BUSINESS
FACES
the
URBAN
CRISIS

 gulf publishing company

houston, texas

To my wife, Virginia

Acknowledgements: Space doesn't permit the listing here of the scores of people who assisted in the preparation of this book. Many are mentioned in the pages of this volume in connection with their activities in facing the urban crisis. I thank them all. Special thanks go to two not named who provided valued advice and counsel — Edward J. Kneeland and Thomas F. Hilber, Jr., of General Electric.

Contents

Business Faces the Urban Crisis

The Active Volcano

The riots in the cities in the late 1960's made glaringly evident the volcano on which most Americans now live. How can we tame the volcano? How can we put its explosive force to use?

No single institution in our society can harness this cataclysmic energy. But one institution, working in concert with others, may have a chance — business.

Many business leaders are committing their companies to the problems now:

● The late Gerald L. Phillippe when he was board chairman of General Electric Company:

> As a nation, I believe, we are rapidly breaking out of a system that has insisted that social problems were the exclusive province of the government or the theorists. Managers in major corporations today find themselves involved in everything from space exploration to the training and employment of hard-core dropouts in the big city ghettos. On behalf of their organizations, they are building new bridges and relationships with every part of their environment — government, education, labor, and, of course, their customers.

● Board chairman Henry Ford II of Ford Motor Company:

> People who don't face up to this issue are stupid. It's a great opportunity for business. It's shortsighted not to step in and do something to solve the problem.

1

• President Charles B. McCoy of E.I. du Pont de Nemours & Company:

> Obviously, no business can operate successfully, over a long period of time, in a crumbling social structure....We must try to respond. As I see it, we can do so in two ways. First, we can encourage the employees of business organizations to become more involved as individuals in the solution of community problems. Second, where there are reasonable ways for us to mesh our corporate resources with the needs of society, we can offer corporate assistance.

• President Sterling Tooker of Travelers Insurance Company:

> The much greater recognition that all groups in our society now have of the scope and seriousness of urban ills should eventually create an atmosphere more conducive to devising effective long-range solutions.

• David Rockefeller, board chairman of the Chase Manhattan Bank of New York:

> Our central cities are crucial to the economic health of our nation. The same successful managerial techniques which have been applied to our businesses must be brought to bear when dealing with our social problems.

While other business leaders express similar sentiments, does agreement come from spokesmen for Negroes?

• Whitney M. Young, Jr., executive director of the National Urban League:

> [No institution] is better equipped to exercise effective leadership and turn America around than the business community. Businessmen are the status symbols, the role models, the community leaders, the image-makers....[They] cannot enjoy the prestige and the status and the leadership...without at the same time assuming responsibility for the negative by-products of the system.

• Robert C. Weaver, secretary of Housing & Urban Development in President Johnson's Cabinet:

We must explore new ways of more fully utilizing the managerial expertise. . .of the private sector in this undertaking.

• Dr. Kenneth B. Clark, president of the Metropolitan Applied Research Center in New York, professor of psychology at City College of New York, consultant to the National Association for the Advancement of Colored People, research psychologist for the Carnegie Corporation:

> Business and industry are our last hope. They are the most realistic elements of our society. Other areas in our society — government, education, churches, labor — have defaulted in dealing with the Negro problems. It is now up to business. Other elements can lose in terms of guilt or conscience. But business has profits to lose also. It has efficiency to lose, economy and, of course, it has tremendous investments it can lose unless there is lasting racial peace. Stability is essential to the kind of industrial and economic system which we have.

• Frank Ditto, a black militant leader in Detroit:

> If you cats [businessmen] can't do it, it's never going to get done. The government can't lick this problem. So business has to.

In commenting on the role of business in helping to solve the urban crisis, *Fortune* devoted an issue to the subject in January, 1968, and editorialized:

> Of course, the more congealed liberals. . .whose opinions on this subject entered a zone of permafrost in the 1930's, continue to doubt that business can be the agent of the kind of social advance that is needed. But the leaders of the government of the U.S. believe it. Negroes believe it. Business is the one important segment of society Negroes today do not regard with bitter disillusionment. And thousands of businessmen across the nation, getting involved in the struggle to restore social cohesions, are beginning to lift their sights, to sense that business has indeed a great part to play.

Two Crises in One

We face two related problems, not one. The first is the Negroes' struggle for equality. It happens to coincide with — and is aggravated by — a broader crisis in our urban life. That crisis shows most dramatically in the riots in Los Angeles, Detroit, Cleveland, Newark, and other cities, but it existed before the riots, and it will remain even if riots subside.

New York City's annual slum bill, for example, is $3.2 billion. Welfare alone costs $1.5 billion — $1 billion in federal and state funds, plus $500 million raised by the city. To that, add a $1.7 billion subsidy in the taxes that the slums don't pay, the extra fire and police protection they require, and the social and health problems they create.

Yet even that enormous expenditure doesn't do the job. According to the New York Regional Planning Association, the city needs another $1.1 billion each year — $300 million for educating slum children, plus $800 million for a myriad of poverty services.

Is New York unique among American cities? No, although it probably is an advanced example of what we can expect to happen in other U.S. cities in less than a decade if the tide is not turned. Today, in a period of prolonged prosperity and shrinking poverty, welfare payments in the nation exceed $5 billion a year. About 9 million Americans are on relief — more than in 1940, the terminal year of the depression.

Nor does welfare tell the full story. An estimated 5 million urban homes are in disrepair. City crime rates are up 44 per cent in the last five years. About 1 million young people were school dropouts in 1965, and that figure has improved only moderately since then.

Yet even the dismal statistics on slums, welfare, housing, crime, and school dropouts don't measure the full dimensions of the urban crisis. America has become an urban civilization — a nationwide complex of core cities, satellite cities, suburbs, and towns.

This urban giant has grown like weeds with little planning while most Americans' attention for the past 50 years has focused on matters such as federal and international affairs. Below the international and federal levels, the troubles have heated to a boil — at the weakest and most neglected points in our governmental system. Things have grown so bad that Robert Weaver has wondered, in public, why anyone would ever want to become mayor of a major American city.

Nearly all city administrators face financial difficulties, both because of their expensive problems of crime, education, welfare, public health, and housing and because the people and businesses who can afford to pay the taxes are fleeing the core cities – leaving a steadily rising percentage of the poor who cannot.

The Rural Impact

Ironically, the rural areas – especially the rural South – have contributed importantly to the crisis in the cities. More than 1 million Southern Negroes have migrated to Northern cities in the past decade, even though they know they leave the rural peace and quiet for the urban stew and turmoil. About 100,000 came North in 1968 – most of them practically penniless, many functionally illiterate, and few with trades or skills that command more than the minimum wage.

Yet they continue to migrate because they have little choice. If good jobs are hard to find in the cities, they often don't exist in the country, especially in the South. Since World War II, mechanization has revolutionized Southern farming. Machines have been inexorably supplanting thousands of hired hands and sharecroppers on cotton plantations, tobacco lands, and corn-fields.

In 1966, the median income for Negro families in Southern states and the District of Columbia was $3,422. In the rest of the U.S., median Negro family income was $5,746. Three houses out of four occupied by Negroes in small towns and rural areas of the South are without basic plumbing or are dilapidated – or both. In the large cities of the North and West, only 15 per cent of Negro homes are in such condition. (*The South* is defined as the eleven states of the Confederacy, plus Kentucky and Oklahoma.) The Southern educational system has left 33.5 per cent of adult Negroes illiterate, and of course almost unemployable. In the rest of the nation, the illiteracy proportion for Negroes is 23.4 per cent.

In the past generation, when 3.5 million Negroes have fled North and West, they headed principally for major cities such as New York, Cleveland, Detroit, Chicago, and Los Angeles, but now they go more to the smaller cities. In 1940, one Southerner in four was black; today only one in five is. Seventy-seven per cent of all U.S. Negroes lived in the South in 1940; now only slightly more than half do.

The rural impact on the cities comes in other ways, too, and it began long before the crisis in race relations. From the days of the first colonists, Americans have not esteemed the urban life or made folk heroes out of many city dwellers. The eccentric Johnny Appleseed is a legend today for his bucolic roamings in Ohio and environs. But who ever developed a song or legend about the far more important Moses Cleaveland who founded Cleveland, the first major city in the U.S. to elect a Negro mayor? Even the residents apparently did not hold their founder in sufficient regard to maintain the same spelling for their city's name.

From the days of Thomas Jefferson to now, myths, legends, songs, novels, plays, and advertisements extol the rural life and rarely praise the urban. One effect of this has been to politically institutionalize the myth — for example, in continuing federal farm subsidies while cities struggle for state and U.S. funds; in a Department of Agriculture established in 1862 but a Department of Housing and Urban Development not created until 1965; and in disproportionate political power among rural voters.

The generally prevailing myth goes something like this: The nation was founded, colonized, and pioneered by the *good guys* like John Alden, Daniel Boone, and Davy Crockett — rural types to the man. It was exploited by the *bad guys* like Boss Tweed, Samuel Insull, and Al Capone — urban types to the core.

Americans have never really trusted the city. Because of that pervading mistrust and because of the traditional eulogy to the rural life, America — until recently — has given its cities only incidental attention.

The Phenomenon of Expectations

The riots have awakened us to the plight of our cities. Yet, why didn't they occur much sooner? Contemporary accounts of

Harlem in the 1920's indicate conditions were as bad then as now – and possibly worse. No widespread riots occurred there then, and usually a man could safely walk the streets at night.

Dr. Robert N. McMurry, an industrial psychologist, attributes the rioting to changing mores which condone greater permissiveness and violence. Probably some of the rioting does stem from permissiveness and the fact that relatively few of the rioters have been caught and even fewer seriously punished.

But the Negro psychologist, Dr. Kenneth Clark, draws attention to a striking and disturbing fact. The major riots of the late 1950's and 1960's all followed the passage of each of the federal civil-rights laws. Furthermore, almost every one of the cities in which urban eruptions have occurred are in states – California, Michigan, Ohio, New York, and New Jersey – which have strong civil-rights laws, strong fair-employment statutes, and strong open-occupancy requirements.

In *The Ordeal of Change*, stevedore-philosopher Eric Hoffer points out that people with no hope seldom revolt. When they get a little hope, then "the phenomenon of expectations" comes into play. They want more freedom, prosperity, or whatever else they believe has been denied them.

When deprived minorities get a taste of equality, they want more. When they don't get more, they become increasingly frustrated, to the point of rioting. The phenomenon of expectations even proves powerful enough to lead to riots in slumless centers such as Nyack, New York, Fort Lauderdale and Lake Geneva, Florida.

Challenge to Business Effectiveness

Within the past ten years, then, America has experienced a crescendo of inner-city violence, an intensity of disruption, and a growth in the duration of the disruption. People sentenced to live in the ghettos of large American cities are randomly and spasmodically rebelling and resisting and are using the disruptive techniques and methods of destroying property and inviting destruction of themselves.

What are these series of urban disturbances telling us? That our techniques of dealing with the problems of the cities no longer work. The requirements of industrial, business, and commercial efficiency are inconsistent with urban instability. We have reached a point where the business and industrial community must ask itself: How do we help remedy this situation, if for no other reason than to have within our cities the conditions essential for business effectiveness?

The present social and racial arrangements are wildly inefficient and uneconomical. They put excessive economic burdens on the business and industrial community. They exclude a significant percentage of human beings from the consumer market who are also underutilized as labor. Because of the present racial arrangements in America, about 10 per cent of the population is an underdeveloped segment of the society. The gross national product is therefore arbitrarily and unnecessarily limited and retarded because a potentially efficient society has not adjusted itself to efficient use of human resources. This seems particularly paradoxical in the light of U.S. activities since World War II to help the rest of the free world to develop itself under the Marshall Plan and other programs.

Government and Philanthropy to the Rescue?

Attempts to solve the urban crisis have not worked. Neither public nor private philanthropy has relieved the situation. As social service agencies and settlement houses have increased in number, in staff, and in budget, the pathology of our cities has increased at an even greater rate.

The judicial branch of the federal government has played a vital role in removing the legal basis for racial segregation in America, but it has not by itself been able to find the formula to translate its decisions into social change and progress. Between the 1950's and 1960's the legislative branch of the federal government has passed civil-rights legislation which even the most optimistic Negro observer of the 1950's would not have expected until at least the 1980's. Although aid-to-cities legislation has fallen short of what some urban experts advocated, the help voted has nevertheless proved substantial. But again, the frustrating fact remains that the futilities of life in the ghettos did not change significantly.

The executive branch has vigorously administered the judicial rulings and the enacted legislation relating to the urban crisis. In addition, President after President has supported reform in word and deed. Nevertheless, the urban crisis continues and may even worsen.

The National Commission on Urban Problems released a study in July, 1968, showing that, with current trends, "America by 1985 would be well on the road towards a society characterized by race stratification along racial and economic lines as well as geographic separation." The analysts were projecting present, measurable trends, not making unsubstantiated predictions.

According to the projections, the population of metropolitan areas having 50,000 or more will have increased by 58 per cent from 1960 to 1985. The central cities will have increased within present boundaries by only 13 per cent, but the suburban ring will have more than doubled.

Nonwhites will increase in numbers at a greater rate throughout the nation than whites, their proportion of the total population rising from 11 per cent in 1960 to 14 per cent in 1985.

But in the central cities the increase of nonwhites is expected to be even greater. Central cities were 82 per cent white and 18 per cent nonwhite in 1960. By 1985, according to the projections, the white population will have dropped to 69 per cent and the nonwhite population increased to 31 per cent, with many major cities having nonwhite majorities. Although nonwhites were expected to increase numerically in the suburbs from 2.8 million in 1960 to 6.8 million in 1985, the study said they "will still be all but lost in a sea of whites, with the nonwhite suburban population increasing only from 5 to 6 per cent of the total."

Paul H. Douglas, former senator from Illinois and chairman of the commission, said:

> This is hard reality we must face. I am not as optimistic as I was six months ago.

The objective of this volume is twofold: to show how business is beginning to play its role and to explore new or emerging dimensions of the part it must enact. The thesis of this book is that not all is lost, that hope for a solution exists with businessmen. Evidence that a growing number of them think so, too, lies in results of surveys by an industrial pulse-taker.

In January, 1967, these two questions were posed to executives in 700 major American corporations:

1. Should your company be active in the broad area of social problem-solving?
2. If so, does your company have the knowledge and personnel required to successfully launch and maintain action programs?

In 1967, 42 per cent answered "yes" to the first question; only 14 per cent (or 6 per cent of the total polled) were confident that they knew how and where to act.

The same two questions were repeated early in 1968. Significantly, 82 per cent of the corporate leaders said their companies should be active; 29 per cent were confident that they knew how to get their company involved.

Two points stand out about the two surveys: In only 12 months the number of companies which had decided that they should be involved doubled; and there is still a large gap between the commitment to act and the knowledge of how to do so.

What Can Business Do?

If government and philanthropy have not come up with creative solutions to the urban crisis, why should anybody expect business and industry to be able to? Perhaps it's because nearly everything else has failed and business represents, in the words of psychologist Kenneth Clark, the "last hope."

In an April, 1966, study by Opinion Research Corporation of 23 industrial communities, 600 community leaders saw some role for business in dealing with virtually every community problem. Over 60 per cent responded positively to the question, "Should companies become involved in *all* community problems?" Community leaders say that fear of being called *paternalistic* is no reason to stay out of community affairs. Only in the areas of racial conflict and partisan politics did even as many as one in ten say business should keep hands off.

But other observers advise a more restrained and balanced approach. For example, Du Pont's Mr. McCoy says:

> We must be realistic. Like any type of organization, business faces some limits. We have no right and no desire to impose our will on the community. We want to help, but not to control, and we cannot do everything at once.
>
> All of us have to live with priorities. It is an unpleasant responsibility, for so much needs doing, and we wish we could do it all at once. But

11

we cannot. To back one proposal means rejecting another. For every program that is launched, we can point to another need left unfilled.

Why Face the Urban Crisis?

The Opinion Research study reports that community relations specialists in companies that have achieved high community standing give the following reasons why more attention to solving local problems has become a business necessity:

1. Social problems affect business. An office equipment manufacturer says, "Problems like zoning, water supply, and traffic improvement obviously relate to the success of our business as well as to the community."
2. When business doesn't act, the government does. An eastern telephone company representative comments, "Somehow leaders of economic enterprises have not provided enough solutions to problems like education and care of the aged. So we get 'Great Society' legislation."
3. There is danger of restrictive legislation. A basic steel producer says, "If companies don't do something about air and stream pollution, restrictive legislation will result."
4. A good community is necessary to attract and hold employees. An electrical equipment manufacturer states, "We have a definite responsibility on pollution and equal job opportunities. Also to attract and retain top engineering talent, we need a progressive community."
5. Success depends on attracting industry. An electric utility spokesman says, "Our business success is tied up with the success of the community. What's good for the community is good for us."
6. An improved community life helps business. "The purpose of taking part in local affairs is not just for the good of the company," points out an office equipment producer. "We encourage people because we think everyone should be interested in improving his community."

Henry Ford II probably summed up the consensus among businessmen when he told Ford Motor Company stockholders in May, 1968:

Your company and members of its management are engaged in such [ghetto-area] activities because we believe that business and industry have an obligation to serve the nation in times of crisis, whether the danger is internal or external. It is clear, moreover, that whatever seriously threatens the stability and progress of the country and its cities also threatens the growth of the economy and your company. Prudent and constructive company efforts to help overcome the urban crisis are demanded not only by your company's obligations as a corporate citizen but by your management's duty to safeguard your investment.

The relevant question about the increasing efforts of business to seek solutions to the urban crisis is not, should it participate in such ventures? Rather, it is, how should it participate?

Business Schools on Urban Course

How do business schools regard participation? They are often in the vanguard of thinking about new frontiers for management.

Harvard Graduate School of Business Administration and other leading institutions are striving to find ways to better prepare their students for the new roles corporate executives are increasingly being called on to play in easing the nation's racial crisis and other urban problems.

The schools are adding new, socially oriented courses to their curricula and are emphasizing racial and urban matters in existing courses.

Cyril C. Ling, executive secretary of the American Association of Collegiate Schools of Business, says:

The federal government's push to get businessmen involved in these problems is stimulating a real interest on the part of business schools to get out onto the firing line with the companies.

Deans and professors at the University of Pennsylvania Wharton School of Finance and Commerce, the Stanford University Graduate School of Business, Massachusetts Institute of Technology Alfred P. Sloan School of Management and elsewhere are quick to point out that they long have been dealing with ethical and social questions in their regular classes. They concede, however, that probably far too little emphasis was given to such topics until recently. One Harvard professor says:

> Five years ago very little was said in class about corporate social responsibilities or environmental pollution or the city's ills; and the only time we did talk about such subjects, it was in terms of how businessmen could fit in without rocking the boat.
>
> Now enrollment is falling off considerably in such courses as production, technical aspects of management and economics, and it's increasing in the socially oriented courses. Any course that has the word "urban" in its title is just swamped with enrollments.

Walter Fackler, acting dean of the University of Chicago Graduate School of Business, says:

> It's difficult to know what we should be doing. We're getting all sorts of requests for all sorts of involvement. We're groping for criteria to help us decide what kinds of things the business school should get into and what things we're going to have to leave for others to do.

What Effects on Business and Society?

Groping appears to be the operative word in grappling with the urban crisis. One reason for the groping lies in concern about the possible effects that industry's urban ventures may have on business and society.

Hazel Henderson, a founder of Citizens for Clean Air Inc., a member of the New York Business Council for Clean Air, and also a member of the Welfare Advisory Board of the New York Junior League, gave voice to those fears in an article in the July-August 1968 issue of *Harvard Business Review:*

> Companies from AT&T to Xerox have been urged — and in many cases have willingly accepted — the challenges [sic] to educate our children, police our streets, clean up our polluted air and water, teach our disadvantaged citizens how to earn a living, rebuild our slums, and even tell us how to run our cities more efficiently. If this trend continues, how will private enterprise itself change? What kind of changes will this trend bring about in our ways of doing things in society as a whole?

Will government get smaller as it unloads burdens it has been unable to cope with onto industry? Will corporations grow still bigger and become more like charitable foundations?

The turn to industry to help solve urban problems, long thought to be the private preserve of government, is not as surprising as it may at first appear. The 50 largest U.S. corporations own over half of all manufacturing assets in America, and the 500 largest own more than two-thirds. General Motors took in revenues in 1966 that exceeded the annual gross national product of all but 13 of the free-world nations.

Industry has the material resources to turn loose on urban problems. In defense and space work it has brilliantly demonstrated that it can work closely with government. But even while businessmen begin to try to cope with the *how* of solving urban problems, they also worry about the effect such efforts will have on the nature of their organizations and on society generally.

In the area of organization, they foresee the need for more reliance on the social sciences if they want to learn to deal with environmental problems. Some shy away from that, perhaps because of disagreeable experiences when they have dabbled in this field previously. But not all do. For example, Ben S. Gilmer, president of American Telephone and Telegraph, says:

There are those in our business who see the need for nothing less than carefully organized, definitely expert social research that will keep us fit to anticipate, or at the very least keep up with, rapid changes in the environment that could otherwise leave a business wondering what in the world hit it. Fifty or more years ago industry started moving in a substantial way toward research in the natural sciences. Out of this move, and the union of science and technology, came the advances that have produced both the benefits and also some of the problems we have today. Today, half a century later, the time may well be at hand when a business that hopes to survive and prosper will have no less a need for social and environmental research and planning than it had in the past for technical insights and expanding technical proficiency.

So, perhaps the enforced reliance on social scientists will bring unforeseen benefits to industry in its business planning, just as its enforced reliance on natural scientists has brought technological rewards not envisioned at the beginning of this century.

Another organizational concern centers around the forms a business enterprise may take when it finds itself heavily involved in urban affairs. Will government demand great control of such a company, even to the extent of a partial ownership that turns it into a government-supervised utility? This has already happened with many enterprises in Western Europe, even if they don't do substantial business with the government.

Or will new companies, partially government-owned and partially privately owned, be formed for radically new ventures — to plan, develop, and build completely new cities, for example much as Comsat was established for the communication satellite business?

Or will the existing organizational structure not change significantly? Will companies take urban work on a contract basis, just as they do most of the space and defense work now?

Nobody can predict precisely how business organization will change. Yet industry has met the challenge of defense and space work with only evolutionary shifts in structure, largely to take better advantage of natural science and to cooperate more effectively with the federal government. The odds are that the same evolutionary developments will occur as business works more closely with local government.

Hazel Henderson appears to favor the contract method when business participates in urban projects:

> The safest way to turn any public problem over to private industry is to (a) let out a government contract, with all the specifications carefully set down in writing and (b) pay a fair price, as in the case of space and military programs. This may cost a little more, but it would be worth it in the long run.

The contract route would also help safeguard the public against some well meaning corporate chief, who, in deciding what is good for our society, would turn into a benevolent, paternalistic ruler.

A few businessmen have expressed another kind of fear — that they will be the victims of a Negro backlash if they try to help and fail. The only answer to that lies in the analogy of the buggy whip manufacturer who recognized the obsolescence of his product but made no effort to produce anything more modern for fear of failure.

Groping for the "How"

While the groping continues on the philosophical level, it also goes on at a more hectic pace at the pragmatic level of finding immediate solutions to immediate urban problems. But before you take up specific projects, businessmen known for their leadership in community affairs suggest that you consider these guidelines to help orient yourself, both as to how much your company is equipped to take on and as to the nature of the problems in your community:

1. What is your company participation now?
   Learn if employees, particularly key executives, are already working on the problems most important to your company.
2. How deeply is your company committed?
   Company representatives must be decision makers who can speak for the company and make commitments.
3. Have you resources of untapped executives?
   Firms now active on community problems report that executives are more willing to participate than is usually thought.
4. What is the priority for community problems?
   You can identify important problems through formal community studies and discussions with community leaders in education, politics, labor, and business.
5. What is the local climate for business?
   Make a regular and systematic study of the local labor, educational, tax, and political situation to pinpoint potential problems.
6. Can and should you support other leaderships?
   One company can't do it all. Management should be prepared to back other leaders working on problems important to the company.
7. Is the local top executive used where he will do the most good?

It's usually better to concentrate one top executive's activities so that he can make a meaningful contribution to one or two important projects than to scatter his effort.

8. Are you in touch with emerging community leaders?
Leadership varies, depending on the problem. Seek out the real leaders in each situation. Do not deal only with *traditional* leaders.

Once you have an overview of your situation, you may be appalled at the complexities and difficulties that face you. Take solace in and advantage of assets you may have overlooked:

1. Modern corporations are flexible and innovative. They are accustomed to sensing and meeting and evoking the changing desires of the public. Above all, they practice the difficult art of mobilizing specialized knowledge for action — the art of mediating progress, of managing change.

2. Business has long and deep experience with customers. Think of the cities as customers, albeit specialized, and apply to urban *clients* the customer-relation techniques that have long worked well with more conventional buyers of your goods and services.

3. Many companies have already had extensive experience with the federal government as a buyer. Apply the knowledge learned there to the local levels. Many companies have long sold to cities the conventional products local governments need. Apply that knowledge to selling the more unusual services required today.

4. Business, the city, and the Negro are all victims of the agrarian myth over the American mind. Black people may already sense this. At least the opinion polls indicate that they accord business the highest marks of any American institution today. By publicly taking its stand on the side of the city and the Negro, business can help improve its own reputation and its internal morale. Today's indictment of business has its roots in the agrarian bias against bigness, not in belief that business exploits the poor. Business is already essentially an urban institution. It depends largely on the city populations for both its markets and its labor force. The

Negro and the city — the twin elements of the broader urban crisis — are already businessmen's potential allies.

So, with these *hidden assets*, you at least have a leg up in developing ways and means to help solve the urban crisis — the nitty gritty of most of this volume.

The Method of This Book

As Du Pont's Mr. McCoy and many others point out, business cannot and should not try to participate in every kind of urban project. Rather, it should concentrate on the areas where it already has some measure of expertise. The following represents areas where many businesses can contribute:

- Revising hiring and recruiting practices to increase employment.
- Training the unemployed or underemployed.
- Solving three social environmental problems.
- Coping with the promise and peril of black capitalism.
- Applying technology to environmental problems.
- Helping grass-roots government grow healthier.
- Making corporate philanthropy more effective.
- Dealing with civil disturbance.

The remainder of this book will consist of case studies in each of the eight areas, with an analytical chapter following each set of examples suggesting how you may apply and adapt them to your circumstances. Each analytical chapter will include extensive checklists to facilitate such application and adaptation.

The instances which follow by no means exhaust all the stories of what industry is doing in any of the eight areas. They were selected because they were typical, adaptable, or novel — or a combination of those qualities.

3 Integrating Your Work Force

The National Planning Association estimated the need for almost 14 million more workers than U.S. Labor Department data indicate will make up the American employed work force by 1975 — if we keep alive our aspirations as a nation for better health, education, housing, social welfare, and urban development.

In the planning association's study, *Manpower Requirements for National Objectives in the 1970's,* prepared for the Department of Labor's Manpower Administration and published in February, 1968, these points stand out about manpower change by 1975 which relate to work-force integration:

1. The 1965-1975 decade will witness a rise of about 20 per cent in the U.S. labor force. The net increase will amount to about 15 million workers — the largest upturn for any ten-year period in American history.
2. A big part of the 1965-1975 story lies in the radically different pattern of change which will occur among the various age groups. One age group — those who will be between 35 and 44 years old — will experience a decline of about 1 million by 1975. The adjacent age group — those between 25 and 34 years — will rise by an unprecedented 6 million, or 40 per cent, double the overall rate of labor-force increase.

3. Highlighting these changes will be the enormous differential between white and nonwhite increases in the labor force by 1975. Because of the postwar bulge in birth rates, the number of new, nonwhite workers will increase by more than 50 per cent. Nonwhites below 25 years of age will make up one of every seven workers in the U.S. All employers searching for manpower, especially in the face of the projected decline among the more experienced adult workers, are already finding – and will find it more so in the immediate years ahead – that the pool of available workers is made of the younger age groups in which nonwhites account for increasingly significant numbers.

4. This manpower profile comes in the face of projected changes in the kinds of jobs available. Seymour L. Wolfbein, dean of Temple University's School of Business Administration, predicts that by 1975:

- Less than 5 per cent of all workers will be producing all the agricultural yield in this country.
- About one of every two people who work will be engaged in white-collar occupations.
- One of every seven workers will be professional personnel.
- Professional personnel will, for the first time, outnumber the skilled craftsmen, the historic symbol of American enterprise.
- Less than 5 per cent of all workers will be unskilled.

5. Great changes are coming in the city manpower profile, on top of the dramatic shifts that have already occurred. For example:
- Between 1965 and 1970 the Negro population in central cities will rise by 20 per cent; it will fall by 1 per cent among the whites.
- Yet job opportunities are steadily moving outside the central city, especially among those industries and occupations which have experienced (and are expected to continue to in the years ahead) the largest overall growth rates.

6. A considerable part of the urban poor, particularly the
nonwhites, are recent arrivals from rural poor America. With
a total U.S. population increase of 28 million from 1955 to
1965, the rural population actually declined by 400,000 — all
of it and more accounted for by a drop of 600,000 among
Negro rural residents.

Most of those leaving are younger workers (for years, the
highest migration rates have prevailed among people in their late
teens and twenties). The Department of Agriculture predicts a
migration rate as high as 35 per cent among that part of the rural
labor force which will be made up of those in their twenties during
the 1965-1975 decade.

The Unemployed, the Underemployed

With the foregoing six observations as background, we're ready
to see that the poor in general, the nonwhite in particular, and the
urban ghetto resident especially, have experienced: the highest
rates of unemployment and the highest incidence of underemployment.

In terms of unemployment, Table 3-1 tells the story. Sustained
rates of economic growth and even overall employment growth
have failed to make a meaningful dent on the extremes in
unemployment.

Data for 1967 show that:

• In the 20 largest standard metropolitan statistical areas, the
unemployment rates are higher for the central city than for the
urban fringe.

• The unemployment rates are considerably higher for nonwhites than for whites.

• The unemployment rates are consistently much higher for
the nonwhites in their teens than for the whites in their teens, as
shown in Table 3-2.

In general, the 1967 unemployment rates for the central cities
were 43 per cent higher than the corresponding rates for their
outlying urban areas. Unemployment rates of these central cities

Table 3-1

Differentials in Unemployment Rates in 1967

National average	3.8%
Men in professional and technical work	1.3
Married men	1.8
Whites	3.4
Nonwhites	7.4
Men in unskilled occupations	7.5
18- and 19-year-old boys	10.5
18- and 19-year-old girls	12.7
16- and 17-year-old boys	14.5
16- and 17-year-old girls	14.8
Nonwhite 18- and 19-year-old boys	20.1
Nonwhite 18- and 19-year-old girls	28.3
Nonwhite 16- and 17-year-old boys	28.9
Nonwhite 16- and 17-year-old girls	32.0

Table 3-2

1967 Unemployment Rates in the 20 Largest Areas

	Central Cities	Urban Fringes
Total	4.7%	3.3%
White	3.7	3.1
Nonwhite	7.6	7.0
White men 20 years and over	2.8	1.7
Nonwhite men 20 years and over	4.9	4.4
White women 20 years and over	3.5	3.6
Nonwhite women 20 years and over	6.6	6.3
White persons 16 to 19 years old	11.5	10.7
Nonwhite persons 16 to 19 years old	31.6	37.5

were 24 per cent higher than the corresponding rates for the nation.

In terms of underemployment, consider the fact that while just about one out of every two white workers is in a white-collar job, the corresponding ratio among nonwhites is about one in five. The proportion of whites in professional jobs is double that of the nonwhites.

Our work force is changing. We are experiencing a severe labor shortage, especially for skilled and white-collar people. The great untapped reservoir of people is among nonwhites, particularly those in the central cities. American employers must integrate their work forces out of necessity, not for idealistic reasons. Studies show that those companies which emphasize the moral aspects of racial integration generally accomplish the least.

Nor can legislation truly accomplish real integration. As is so often the case, laws may eventually prove almost superfluous. (For the record, the most important federal statute is Title VII of the Civil Rights Act of 1964, which applies to every employer with more than 25 employees. It is administered by the Equal Employment Opportunity Commission. Most employers who contract with the federal government are covered by Executive Order 11246 relating to equal employment, administered by the Labor Department's Office of Federal Contract Compliance.)

Jobs Go Begging

In May, 1968, New York City wrestled with the paradox that it had 20,000 unfilled jobs in area businesses at the same time that 135,000 people were registered as unemployed.

The apparent contradiction — that jobs go begging while job-seekers remain idle — highlights a fundamental aspect of New York's, or any city's, employment situation. The available jobs and the available workers do not fit each other, so creating more jobs will not necessarily absorb the unemployed.

The available job may demand more skill, or a different skill, than the worker has. The job may be unattractive to any worker regardless of skill because of low pay, undesirable hours, or unpleasant working conditions. Or the unemployed person may be uninterested in working or satisfied with what income he gets from welfare or unemployment benefits.

American employers are fortunate, not unfortunate, that a sizable, untapped supply of labor still exists. The problem is to find the potentially efficient people, recruit them, train them, and keep them on the job. Examples follow of how business and industry accomplish this.

Chrysler's Experience

Chrysler Corporation discovered the real dimensions of the hard-core unemployment problem when it agreed to train 750 people in that category. Says Chrysler president Virgil B. Boyd:

> I thought I knew what "hard core" meant until we became involved in this area. I was wrong. Hard core refers not to those without steady jobs, but to those who are not equipped for any jobs; not the unemployed, but the unemployable — those who are unable to fill out even a simple job application.
>
> And it goes much deeper than that. For example, some of these people signed on for job training — with an 'X' of course — but failed to show up. And many of those who did report were very late.
>
> As we registered those who did report, we found that many of them had no social security number, had never been counted in a census, or registered to vote, or belonged to any organization of any kind. In most of the accepted senses, they really didn't even exist.
>
> A lot of people in my company . . . were more than ever convinced that many of the people who aren't working just don't want to work. Given the evidence available to them, this was a reasonable conclusion. These people were not only offered jobs, but the offers were made right on their own blocks, or at the favorite corner for standing on, or in the church basement, or the poolroom. So if they didn't show up, they didn't really want to work. It would have been — it always has been — very easy and very defensible to let it go at that.

Mr. Boyd said that a follow-up effort to find out why those who signed on for the program suddenly "dropped out" indicated deeper reasons, however:

If you can't read, how do you know what it says on the destination
signs of the many buses that go by on a given busy street? And a grown
man isn't going to get on — and be sent off — the wrong bus very many
times before he stops getting on buses any more.

Chrysler's follow-up men had to show these people, "one by one,"
how to recognize the proper bus and, in some cases, how and
where to transfer.

Mr. Boyd explains the next step:

At this point, they all knew how to get there, but a significant number
of them continued to be late. It didn't take long to establish another
fact — only one in five owned an alarm clock. Why? Because they'd
never had to be any particular place at any particular time before.

Not only were these people shown how to get to work, but why
they should work:

We took them into the plants and showed them men, just like
themselves, who owned cars, and clothes, and houses, and told them
that they owned them because these men lived within the rules of an
industrial society and showed up for work on time every day.

What really changed the attitudes of the skeptics at Chrysler,
Mr. Boyd adds, was that,

Once the hard-core people knew how, and why, to come to work their
attendance and tardiness record was 500 per cent better than the
average of all our employees.

Of the first 44 hard-core employed by Chrysler, the corporation
lost only one.

Chrysler learned other lessons from its initial efforts. Rejection
of hard-core job applicants for physical reasons, for example, ran
one in five. Of these, 40 per cent were rejected because of poor
vision:

After these rejects were sent to the proper agencies, were tested and
fitted for glasses, our people found that many of them could very
quickly pick up the elementary reading skills required for simple jobs.

The Chrysler company also found that although the majority of the hard-core people had only third- or fourth-grade reading ability:

> They . . . fell within a very acceptable I.Q. range. And given sufficient motivation and direction, they performed at the average level within a relatively few weeks.

Mr. Boyd sums up:

> Our people found far fewer hopeless cases than they had expected. The nonperformers are now performing and performing well. And they are devoting hours of their own time to company-conducted sessions after work, on things like personal hygiene and the efficient management of the money they earn. Some of those people who only a few weeks ago couldn't take the right bus to work are sticking around after their shift is over to take lessons in driving — from volunteer Detroit policemen whose shifts also are over — in cars provided by the company.

How To Recruit

The Chrysler experience underscores the first problem in tapping the reservoir of workers among the hard-core unemployed — finding them. Here are ways some employers approached the difficulty:

• More than half a dozen Negro and Spanish-speaking recruiters are used as "walking employment offices" for Pacific Telephone and Telegraph Company. Besides performing their regular jobs, the recruiters go wherever they expect to find hard-core unemployed, including barber shops, poolrooms, bars.

• The Newspaper Agency Corporation, Charleston, West Virginia, owner and publisher of three newspapers, offers free "situation wanted" ads to the unemployed, with an ad-taker available for assistance in writing the ad.

• Flick-Reedy Corporation, Bensenville, Illinois, has outfitted a van to serve as a mobile job-interview-and-hiring center. It visits job centers, agencies, and church and government organizations that will screen applicants for the company.

• In Los Angeles, television station KTTV used a 19-hour
Job-a-thon patterned after the charity telethons to close the
communication gap between the unemployed in the ghettos and
their potential employers. From Friday night to late Saturday
afternoon, viewers were asked to phone in pledges of jobs for the
residents of several low-income areas in the Los Angeles vicinity.
The announced result was 25,000 job opportunities. On Monday
morning, more than 6,100 job-seekers appeared at local state
employment offices in response to the offers.

• One of Inland Steel Company's young Negro personnel
executives hosts a weekly television show called *Opportunity Line*.
This show broadcasts job openings and invites listeners to call for
interviews and possible job placement. The program has met with
remarkable success. In the first 18 months that the show was on
the air, calls totaled 150,000, or an average of 2,000 a week.

• Ford Motor Company used new recruiting and hiring
practices in Detroit's Inner City. Employment offices were set up
in the heart of the slums. Willingness to work took precedence
over lengthy tests as the major criterion for hiring, and written
tests were eliminated. The open-hiring policy was well publicized
to reach the Negro community. Workers who were hired and could
not afford transportation were given bus tickets to tide them over
until the first pay day.

• Discouraged by the high turnover rate in beginning clerical
positions and by the low standards of high-school graduates,
Equitable Life Assurance Society scaled down its conditions for
employment, excluding categorically only those youths with I.Q.'s
less than 90, narcotics addicts, and perverts. The company paid
little attention even to police records. One finding: Unmarried
mothers proved the best motivated of all dropout employees.

• After the Watts riots in Los Angeles, some 50 companies
sent recruiters to the district and induced the California Employment Commission to open a branch there.

• United Airlines sends Negro pilots, stewardesses, and ticket
agents into the ghettos to talk with people. Says Daniel E. Kain,

personnel director for field services: "These people have to taste it, feel it, see it. Otherwise it's a bunch of hot air."

• General Dynamics Corporation sponsored a Job Opportunity Week at its Quincy, Massachusetts, shipyard to recruit members of minority groups. As a result, the company found jobs or eventual training programs for 200 persons. Kenneth I. Guscott, president of the Boston chapter of the NAACP, reports that "the number of minority-group applicants who have been coming to the shipyard on their own has increased by 300 per cent since the recruitment program was held."

• McDonnell Douglas Corporation has developed a slide presentation for predominantly Negro high schools in St. Louis. It shows Negroes working alongside whites at various jobs. McDonnell employs Negroes in 127 job classifications.

• Twenty-five New York-area companies have set up a consortium, Social Research Corporation, which will recruit, train, and place 800 unemployed persons in its member companies. The project was helped into life by a $2.28 million grant from the U.S. Department of Labor. Member companies have job openings in 60 categories. Hope for the program stems from studies made by Herbert M. Greenberg, director of Social Research, which point out that "there is absolutely no difference between the range of ability in the middle class citizen and hard-core unemployed."

• A Job Fair in Houston, aided by National Alliance of Businessmen, placed 3,700 teen-agers in summer positions in just two days.

Many companies think that they must relax their hiring standards and change their hiring practices. Warner & Swasey Company of Cleveland eliminated the usual hiring yardsticks, including testing. Ohio Bell Telephone Company went back over its list of rejected applicants just to hire some who had been considered unqualified.

Not everyone agrees, however, that lower hiring standards are necessary. H.C. (Chad) McClellan of the Los Angeles Management Council tells companies, "Don't hire anyone who doesn't meet your standards. Don't lower your standards — raise theirs." Most businessmen agree, however, with J.A. Nunn, who manages General Electric's personnel practices, when he says, "Let's avoid practices that screen people out. We need practices that screen them in."

Not many employers will eliminate testing in their recruiting practices, but remember that even simple tests may unfairly screen out some good candidates. Ulric Haynes, Jr., a business-oriented Negro who is president of a firm of minority-group employment consultants, Management Formation, Inc., says, "What the concept of aptitude testing ignores is that the prevailing patterns of discrimination exclude minority-group members from the very experiences on which aptitude tests are based."

If you still use selection tests with minority groups, consult the *Guidelines* worked out by the American Psychological Association and by the U.S. Equal Employment Opportunity Commission to offer *culture-free* or at least *culture-fair* tests.

Many employment tests do not validly test the ability to perform on the job. Example: A common aptitude test used in job-screening procedures asks the applicant to spot the defect in a scene pictured in four photographs or drawings. The fourth may depict a living room in which one of the background windows is cracked. The crack may be obvious to someone not used to seeing cracked windows. A cracked window may, however, be a common sight to a hard-core person. These applicants won't identify the defect as readily as the more advantaged applicant.

How To Keep the Hard-Core on the Job

According to the Chrysler experience, once you have recruited a hard-core person, the problem is next to keep him on the job and make him an efficient worker.

In 1966, International Harvester Company launched New Start, a program to employ high-school dropouts. The project was not an outstanding success; only six out of the fifty new workers remained. Undaunted, the company started another New Start in the spring of 1968. By August of that year, the results had turned out differently. Of the 145 men hired — all of them high-school dropouts and most of them members of street gangs — only 17 had quit or been fired.

Hampton McKinney of the Chicago Urban League offers this explanation:

> International Harvester is willing to take a man and qualify him for a job instead of expecting him to be qualified, coiffed and smelling good. This is something most employers have resisted.

William A. Spartin, general supervisor of employment and recruitment, is even more specific:

> We learned two lessons from our previous experience. A high level of supporting services, on and off the job, is necessary, and our own operating management must be given sensitivity training and orientation.

International Harvester asked four community agencies that serve the black man, including the Urban League, to help with supportive follow-up. The supportive services swing into action as soon as the trainee is recruited. A representative telephones him the night before his first day of training. He picks him up in the morning in a company station wagon and hand-delivers him to International Harvester. The company eliminates red tape and puts him on the payroll the first day — at $2.80 an hour training pay — to strengthen the feeling that this is "for real."

With the help of the agencies, Harvester tries to recruit groups of friends rather than single workers, so that they will reinforce each other in an unfamiliar situation. The company serves milk, coffee, and rolls for the first week to get the trainees into the habit of eating breakfast. These are night people who haven't eaten any kind of breakfast in a long time. Harvester emphasizes cleanliness, safety measures, and discipline — strict for such violations as fighting, theft, and gambling, but more relaxed for tardiness and absenteeism. The company does not relax physical or mental health standards.

Instructors for the four weeks of prejob training were all formerly on the production line. One is a graduate of the 1966 New Start. The purpose: Have the instructor as "for real" as possible — similar to the kind of people the trainee will encounter on the regular job.

In the fourth week of the prejob training phase, the trainee gets a volunteer *buddy* from the plant to which he will be assigned. The buddy is responsible for getting the trainee to and from work and for showing him the ropes at the plant during the eight-week, on-the-job training.

Recruits get assigned to plants as close to their homes as possible. In addition, sometimes an entire class of ten will work in the same plant. Mr. Spartin says:

> New Start graduates have better attendance and tardiness records and better relations with management than employees hired the usual way.

Most companies in business and industry today do little about training their present supervisors to be more sensitive to the problems that new hard-core employees face. Chrysler and Harvester, however, found that this was a must.

At Ford Motor Company, a statement urging "full and active support" of the equal-opportunity policy went out from chairman Henry Ford II to 10,000 executives, managers, supervisors, and foremen. Mr. Ford, however, is realistic about the commitment gap between top management and the lower echelons:

> We have a lot of education to do. The guys we hire have to be trained. It's going to take time to work with our supervisors and foremen who may not agree with everything we do.

To heighten awareness among supervisory personnel of the ghetto recruit's problems, some companies use a "sensitivity kit" developed by Human Development Institute, Inc., of Atlanta. The company specializes in what president Jerome I. Berlin calls "scientifically derived training systems." Much of the kit concerns role-playing, wherein white supervisors wearing black masks try to experience the black man's bitterness, frustration, and anger — emotions often intensified on his first job.

The emotional confrontation of role-playing — "physiological disorientation," Dr. Berlin calls it — is the most dramatic exercise in the kit. To perform it, one supervisor wears a white mask;

another, representing the Negro employee, wears a black one. A third supervisor acts as observer and grades his associates by asking questions from a checklist in the kit workbook.

When the role-playing instructions are opened, the drama unfolds. First, the actors try to immerse themselves in their roles. Next, they engage in a brief but specific dialogue. Says Sam, the white supervisor: "Joe, I want to talk to you." Joe, the black employee chronically five minutes late in the morning, answers: "O.K. What's up?" Sam says: "You've already been warned about being late on the job. What seems to be your problem with getting here on time."

From that point, the supervisors ad-lib. The black-masked supervisor is instructed to think the way he believes a Negro new to the job would think. In this example, Joe's reason for tardiness is heavy morning traffic. He can't see catching his bus an hour earlier just to save five minutes. Yet he never has explained his problem to Sam. Now it is at last in the open. After several minutes of heated discussion, Joe agrees to work five minutes into his lunch break to make up for time lost in the morning.

Dr. Berlin thinks that such confrontations — although elementary — are important to the success of sensitizing supervisors:

> They are usually active men. If we just gave them a film and lecture seminar, they would be bored to death, and it would do more harm than good.

During the nine-to-five session, the supervisors are introduced to other situations aimed at helping them understand the psychology of a black worker in unfamiliar surroundings. They must try to put a puzzle together while wearing vision-distorting prism glasses; take "trust walks," in which one supervisor closes his eyes while another leads him around the room; and, without pencil or paper, solve problems a moderator throws at him.

Forrest Schmid, training director of Whirlpool Corporation in St. Paul, Minnesota, believes that the human development kit should *complement* a company's local effort, not substitute for it, and the Human Development Institute agrees. Explains George Bruce, an institute consultant:

> Many people think all they have to do is buy the program for their supervisors and that's the end of it. Not so. This is just an eye-opener, the beginning of the sensitizing process.

When you have strong supportive services (including training) on and off the job and a supervisory force sympathetic to a ghetto resident's problems, you still may not keep the man on the job if the work proves to be beyond his capabilities. You may have to restructure some of your jobs to make them easier to master. Lockheed compares this to methods used to train wartime workers.

Buxton-Skinner in St. Louis established a category of electrician's helper, one step below electrical-maintenance assistant, to provide niches for poorly skilled workers.

To implement its nurses training project, the Kaiser Foundation in San Francisco created the job of clinical assistant to relieve nurses of routine chores such as weighing patients and taking temperatures.

But this approach may not appeal to every company. A manager says:

> McDonnell Douglas in Los Angeles has never changed production procedures to fit trainees. We fit the trainees to our procedures.

McDonnell Douglas doesn't think much of the war-period analogy, either:

> The days of Rosie the Riveter are gone forever. The one-step assembly worker has given way to workers handling a variety of operations requiring a broader knowledge on the production line.

That makes job training the vital link in keeping the ghetto resident on the job. So important is this that the next section is devoted to it.

Here are some other, miscellaneous ways employers keep ghetto residents on the job after the company has recruited them, spoonfed them in the first weeks, sensitized the supervisors to their special problems, and trained them:

• Honeywell, Inc., appointed a full-time transportation coordinator in the Minneapolis area. He found 200 employees willing to organize car pools to help bring ghetto residents to work. In addition, many of the 800 Honeywell employees who already participated in car pools offered to cooperate. The transportation coordinator also worked with the Twin Cities Rapid Transit Company getting bus schedules changed and routes altered to provide public transportation for employees who couldn't drive.

• Early in 1967 two Lockheed Aircraft divisions began experimental programs with these entrance requirements: Candidates *must* be school dropouts, unemployed for most of the last year, have a low yearly income and an unstable work record over the last five years. At least 75 per cent of the trainees must be members of a minority race; 25 per cent must have police records. The idea — that a poor-risk recruit will stay if he is well trained, well paid, and is doing meaningful work — has proved psychologically sound. The turnover rate of employees completing training has been low and performance good.

• Recognizing that present white employees will strongly affect the environment for new black workers, Owens-Illinois, Inc., mounted a vigorous communication program for its white employees, urging understanding and cooperation.

• Southern New England Telephone Company, along with many other companies, runs frequent articles in its employee publication about Negro problems in business. The most common form these stories take is the interview or the case study. The telephone company's interviews are remarkable for their frankness, discussing such normally taboo subjects as prejudice, ("Prejudice at the telephone company is very subtle," one interviewee is quoted as saying), and riots, ("Where were you when four children were blown up? Don't talk to me about riots"). The reason for such articles is summed up in the comment of one black employee of the company: "Negroes and whites don't get enough chance to understand each other. If everybody could sit down and talk like we're doing now, they could understand each other's views and respect each other, and there wouldn't be any trouble."

Where Negro Employment Makes Slow Gains

We have concentrated thus far in this chapter on the subject of employing hard-core minorities. Organizations like the National Alliance of Businessmen have experienced measurable success. But aside from this success, an ironic fact remains. The rate of employment of the better-educated, more advantaged Negroes in business and industry increases only slowly. The better the education and environmental background of the black person, the less relative improvement he appears to be experiencing in gaining a foothold in the business establishment.

In a report on 4,249 New York City businesses, for example, the federal Equal Employment Opportunity Commission found that 43 per cent had no Negro white-collar employees.

The same agency surveyed 100 major New York-based companies that contribute nearly 16 per cent of our gross national product. The study showed that in 1966 Negroes made up only 2.6 per cent of the headquarters staffs of these companies, compared with a citywide average of 5.2 per cent in white-collar job categories. On obtaining 1967 figures for 70 of these corporations before the release of the report, the commission found that they had increased their Negro white-collar forces fractionally, from 2.5 per cent in 1966 to 3.2 per cent.

Although comparable data are not available for white-collar employment of black people in other cities, the odds are high that business and industry does worse outside New York City in this type of minority employment.

Employers are as baffled and frustrated by this lack of good progress on the white-collar front as Negroes themselves.

One solution may be to turn to Negro recruiting organizations. Matching up graduates of Negro colleges with jobs at companies that can't afford to recruit on Negro campuses is a computerized service offered by two young business school graduates.

Thomas H. Main and his Negro roommate, Aaron L. Spaulding, graduates of the Wharton School of Finance and Commerce, have founded Re-Con Services, Inc. They screen black graduates from 80 Negro campuses — mostly in the southeast U.S. — to fill job openings. Re-Con got started with several foundation grants.

Another solution may be training. As a result of advances in training technology, any company, large or small, can readily and successfully conduct a remedial education program to fulfill its needs for reliable, qualified white-collar people, states Nathaniel M. Cartmell, Jr., manager of personnel development for McGraw-Hill, Inc., in New York. Proven materials, methods, and consultants are available to get a company started. "The one essential need is a staff truly in tune with the needs of its trainees," he says. (The next section contains a detailed discussion of white-collar training.)

Yet another solution lies in discarding misleading theories that some white managers have about Negroes. While many managers hold these theories about blacks in general, they apply them frequently to minority people in white-collar jobs. The most prevalent misleading theories are:

1. Customers will not accept Negroes in certain jobs (sales and service, especially).
2. Productivity of whites will drop if they are forced to work beside blacks.
3. Negroes are not dependable.

Such misleading theories have been applied to other minorities, too. In most companies, these theories are untested. Where tested, they have proved unjust.

Throughout this book, most examples of employment and other urban problems involve Negroes bacause black people are far and away the largest segment among nonwhite Americans. Of course, other minorities — notably Puerto Ricans in the East and Mexican Americans in the Southwest — share many of the same urban difficulties that Negroes face.

4 Managing Your Racial Integration

The relation of whites and Negroes is our most grave and perplexing problem . . . . We recommend that employers . . . permit Negroes an equal chance with whites to enter all positions for which they are qualified by efficiency and merit . . . . Especial attention is called to the fact that opportunity is generally denied to Negroes for gaining experience in business methods through service in responsible positions in business houses.

That is not a quotation from the 1968 report of the National Advisory Commission on Civil Disorders. It is from the report of the Chicago Riot Commission of 1919.

Have we made progress in the intervening half-century? "Yes," say some experts. "Very little," say others. Whatever you believe, you will have to acknowledge that the crisis in the cities is as bad now as 50 years ago, and probably worse.

The 1968 Advisory Commission report says that jobs are the "number one problem." Of course, jobs will not automatically halt civil disorders. A majority of those arrested during disorders of the 1960's have been employed. Yet, the existence of high unemployment and underemployment in urban centers has proved a major factor sparking the unrest often started by the more energetic people who have found jobs.

Father Theodore V. Purcell, director of the Cambridge (Massachusetts) Center for Social Studies, comments:

38

With the notable exceptions of the United Packinghouse Workers, the Auto Workers, the American Federation of Teachers, the Transport Workers, and a few others, the unions have done very little. The government has provided leadership with the Civil Rights Act of 1964, the Office of Federal Contract Compliance, the Equal Employment Opportunity Commission, and the fair employment practices commissions of various states. But the practical results of many government commissions have been negligible. The country needs the new force that only business can contribute. It will be healthier for the country if business rather than government becomes "the employer of last resort."

It requires more than gimmickry and tokenism for industry to become truly the "employer of last resort" for minority people. It requires hard thinking, hard planning, and commitment — beginning with the top man in the organization. To manage effectively the full racial integration in your company, take heed of these four guidelines:

1. Examine existing practices.
2. Determine your involvement.
3. Communicate your policy.
4. Set up controls to measure your performance.

Examining Existing Practices

In your self-examination, ask yourself questions such as these:

How many Negro employees do we have? How does the proportion compare with a year ago or five years ago? How does it compare with that of other companies with whom we compete for employees? How does it compare with ratios among competitors in our business? How does it compare with the ratio of Negroes living in the community where we operate?

What jobs do the black employees hold? Do they have strictly *Negro* jobs, such as janitorial work or low-level production tasks? How many perform in white-collar positions? How many as supervisors? As technicians? As managers? How do we stack up with our corporate peers in this regard?

How did we hire our black employees? Did we recruit them actively? Or did they just drift in, starting on low-level jobs? What attitudes do our personnel people have toward Negroes? Do we employ any in personnel? Do we have a program specifically aimed at recruiting blacks? If not, is one necessary? How do records compare on discharges and quits for black and white employees?

Are Negro employees treated differently than whites? Do they use the same facilities? Unofficially, is there a separate seniority roster of Negroes on production jobs? Do certain white-collar jobs bear the unofficial label, For Whites Only? Does the union representing our employees practice subtle discrimination? Are there any Negro stewards or officers? Do any areas in our company have no blacks or, proportionately, far fewer than in others? If so, why?

What skills do our Negro employees possess? How do we know what they have? Do any or many have major skills which we don't use? If so, why? Do many take advantage of our training programs? If not, why? Who, and how many, of the black employees are trainable for higher-rated jobs?

What's the Negro employees' attitude toward the company? Does it differ significantly from that of white employees? Has the attitude changed significantly in recent years? What can we do to improve the attitude? How do the records of black and white employees compare in such areas as efficiency, absenteeism, tardiness, and turnover?

Objective answers to questions such as these may yield unexpected dividends. A Louisville company with Negroes making up a substantial proportion of its hourly employees faced an attempt by a large union to organize all its workers. The union's chief argument was directed to the whites in the unit, playing on their supposed fears that the blacks would somehow jeopardize their jobs. But the personnel manager could find little evidence to support such alarms. He took steps to rectify a situation that his investigations did turn up — the lack of a formal grievance system — and ignored the union's line. The employees voted to remain without a labor organization to represent them.

Determining Involvement

Nobody but extremists would expect you to make your work force all black. You can estimate the extent of your future involvement in racial integration after you answer questions such as the following:

How will our work force change in the future? Will it grow, shrink, remain about the same? How fast will changes occur? When will they take place?

What skills will we require? More in the white-collar area and fewer in blue-collar jobs? What skills won't we require? What are we doing to assure ourselves of people qualified to fill the skills now or eventually to be in short supply? Can Negroes fill some of the skills for which we see a need in the immediate future? What jobs will require skilled people only?

What promotion opportunities exist for present black employees? Does attrition provide most of such promotion chances? Or is it the changing nature of our work? Or our expansion? Can training make more Negro employees promotable? Can we provide training, or is it available outside the company?

What qualifications are required of new employees? Are these qualifications truly relevant, particularly concerning education and experience? How many of our people are now really over-qualified? How many are underqualified? What can we do about those cases, among black or white employees, where the qualifications prove badly out of line with the job requirements?

Every manager should go through such appraisals regardless of considerations about integration. Many who have done so to determine how far they can go in hiring Negroes have found many other shortcomings, too, having nothing to do with the racial mix of their work force.

For example, the production manager for a midwestern maker of office equipment discovered that 45 per cent of his tool and die makers were scheduled for retirement within the next five years. That, plus other normal attrition, meant that he would lose more than half of this skilled group within half a decade. He immediately initiated a training program and took on several Negro apprentices.

Communicating Policy

In determining your involvement, you should also prepare for the difficulties you may encounter with other managers and supervisors in implementing it. But don't overestimate the problems. Be realistic. Set targets. Remember that you can change attitudes. Good communication can do this – letters from the president, stories in the employee paper, boss's speeches, and discussions with especially recalcitrant supervisors. (See, for example, Appendix 1 for the Owens-Illinois communication to its management.)

As indicated in the last chapter with the case of Southern New England Telephone, many companies today also inform their general employees about the dimensions of the urban crisis. Former professional football player Clarence Peaks is on General Electric's payroll in the Philadelphia area, where he tells employees the situation "like it is." He organized a series of seminars on urban problems and race relations. During the summer of 1968, some 130 GE employees and their spouses attended the series on six successive Wednesday evenings in a plant cafeteria.

Topics for discussion included: racial stereotypes, urban black poverty, distortion of the black man's role in American history, creative self- and community-development, the black power movement, black separatism vs. integration, urban-suburban revitalization, industry's responsibility to community development, and areas for cooperative effort. The speakers were local chairmen of civil rights groups, representatives of the Philadelphia Board of Education and other educational organizations.

In evaluating the seminars, Mr. Peaks says:

> The sessions evoked lively (and often heated) discussions and a general feeling among attendees that airing the problems for give-and-take exposure is an early step in improving race relations and solving urban problems.

Sometimes, white employees don't want to hear the message about minority employment. During the 1968 presidential campaign, an Ohio machine tool manufacturer ran a straw vote among its employees for their preferences. A disturbingly high proportion of those voting also took the opportunity to scrawl on the ballots their objections to the company's well-publicized efforts to hire more black employees.

The employer changed the emphasis of its communications, to persuade white employees of the rightness (and legality) of equal employment. "No white worker has yet quit because we're hiring more Negroes," reports the personnel manager.

Setting Up Controls To Measure Performance

Once you have determined your practices, involvement, and communication, you will need controls – periodic reports from managers on:

1. Number of job openings in a period
2. Number of Negroes interviewed
3. Number of Negroes interviewed as a percentage of total hires
4. Number of Negroes hired
5. Number of Negroes hired as a percentage of total hires
6. Number of Negroes promoted or upgraded
7. Number of Negroes trained for specific skills
8. Number of Negroes discharged or who quit – and the reasons

The foregoing four guidelines can help you determine and implement your internal position on work-force integration. But the best planning, communication, and controlling will go for nothing if you can't communicate with the Negro community, if you can't find the blacks to hire, and if you can't keep them aboard once you have recruited them.

Communicating with the Negro Community

The problem of business and industry is still the lack of communication with Negro groups. Although better than it once was, improvement is still needed. Working to improve your rapport with Negro groups can:

• Help your recruiting
• Help your relations with black employees

- Keep the activists from harassing you, especially about the percentages of Negroes in your employ.

Major national groups include the Student Nonviolent Coordinating Committee (SNCC), Congress of Racial Equality (CORE), Urban League, National Association for the Advancement of Colored People (NAACP), the Black Muslims, and the Southern Christian Leadership Conference (SCLC).

But in many areas, the important group is not these but the local groups. Many of the leaders are local officers of national organizations. A good way to spot the best group to deal with is to get in touch with other companies and learn their experiences. Your own Negro employees can also steer you — either indirectly by your observing which organizations they belong to or directly by their giving you their opinions and advice.

Black people in general don't understand how business operates, largely because relatively few blacks have had substantial experience in industrial management positions. This has resulted in unnecessary product boycotts and other unpleasantness.

In one extreme case, a local civil-rights group began boycotting stores selling a particular brand of clothing. Their picket signs read, "Don't buy X sweaters — their maker discriminates against black people." The mystified manufacturer had never had any communication of any sort with the organization.

The placard charges about discrimination came uncomfortably close to the truth, however, so the company decided to ignore the action for awhile, hoping that it would blow over. It did not. Finally, the manufacturer sent an official to see the civil-rights organization. It turned out that the Negro group had confused X brand with the similarly named one of a rival firm which, not surprisingly, hadn't communicated that fact to the protestors.

Many such boycotts have this slap-dash, haphazard quality about them Boycotts have also generally proved ineffective. For the most part, such actions have merely hardened attitudes and made communication more difficult. While boycotts in some cases have led to more employment of minority-group people, the gains have been short-term.

Numerous Negro leaders have come to recognize this. Rev. Leon Sullivan abandoned his boycotting activities in Philadelphia to establish, among other things, Opportunities Industrialization Centers, one of the outstanding Negro-sponsored training efforts in the U.S., with many lines of communication open to industry.

Communication problems also frequently develop because no leader emerges. Somebody often claims leadership, but he can offer little proof that he represents more than a vocal minority of Negroes, Puerto Ricans, or others.

A New England company moved toward solving this problem by holding annual seminars for Negro clergymen, representatives of civil-rights groups, and others with a claim to leadership. "We tell our story," says the company's president, "and we also take the opportunity to do a little educating on business practices." No black people have ever picketed the company, boycotted its products, or come in with demands that it hire more Negroes. Seminar participants, reports the personnel manager, have also referred many good job applicants to it.

A savings and loan bank in New York tried a variation of the New England company's approach after an obscure group presented employment demands to it. It immediately got in touch with all the well-known civil-rights groups and other Negro leaders in its area, presenting its case and offering to consider for employment all qualified Negro applicants. The obscure group quietly withdrew.

But you need to communicate with black youth, too, some of whom you may wish to have working for you some day. Besides contacts in school, you can take advantage of nonschool circumstances. Even tours of your facilities for ghetto youngsters will serve a useful purpose. Normally, however, strive for communication projects with more depth.

The Chase Manhattan Bank launched such a program in 1964, called Business Experience Training (BET). Cooperating with the New York City Board of Education, Chase hires high school juniors and seniors from areas with high dropout rates. The majority are Negroes and Spanish Americans. They work each afternoon from 2 to 5, with time off regularly to attend classes at the bank in the fundamentals of business and finance. If they keep their high school grades up and continue in school until graduation, Chase offers them permanent jobs. Three out of every four of the boys have stayed on after receiving their diplomas. Some are even attending college classes in the evening.

In Pittsfield, Massachusetts, General Electric administers a summer program for junior and senior students of small, predominantly Negro colleges. Students are selected on the basis of their academic and extracurricular achievement and the compatibility of their field of study with specific, full-time summer positions. Plant tours, management and group meetings provide the students with a broad orientation to the industrial environment.

Finding Black Employees

The fundamental truth about recruiting Negroes is this: they tend not to apply for jobs with employers who hire few blacks or only in low-level jobs. You face a severe handicap if you now wish to integrate but have done little thus far. But there's still hope.

Advertise

Primarily use black publications because Negroes seldom read help-wanted ads in "white" dailies.

Despite recruiting efforts of individual firms and the organization of groups of companies to further minority employment, i.e., Plans for Progress, the Urban Coalition, and the National Alliance of Businessmen, Negroes still aren't fully convinced that industry wants them.

Some firms now take an approach that others might emulate. A General Electric ad in *Ebony*, for example, read: "OK, so you're black. We'd like to address you as a man . . . No need to walk on eggs. Or be effusive. Or paternal . . . We simply want to say . . . that there are opportunities here for people with ambition . . . ."

This boldly sympathetic appeal, one of several new approaches in recruitment advertising, gets results. General Electric notes a marked improvement over response to previous ads that took a more conventional line.

Use Local Negro Organizations

The Urban League set up a Skills Bank in many localities in 1963 through a grant from the Rockefeller Foundation. The Rev. Mr. Sullivan's opportunities centers now function in 70 U.S. cities, providing trained Negroes for industrial jobs. The local National Alliance of Businessmen officials can give you good help and advice in the larger American cities.

In addition, more and more local employment agencies are springing up that specialize in minority-group placement. The alliance can aid here, too.

Use Government Organizations

Government groups abound. To help you find your way through the maze, here's a glossary of some of the most important. It's by no means complete, but it will assist you, especially in clarifying the alphabetical confusions.

CAA, CAP — *Community Action Agency* — Contracts with Office of Economic Opportunity to administer community action programs, coordinating practically all federal antipoverty projects in a city or rural area. It's termed Community Action Project in some municipalities.

CAMPS — *Cooperative Area Manpower Planning Systems* — A locally oriented system developed under the Department of Labor in 1967 to meet the need for joint planning and coordinated action in manpower development and related fields. It links federal, state, and local agencies.

JOBS — *Job Opportunities in the Business Sector* — Major federal program to find work for hard-core unemployed. It's sponsored through National Alliance of Businessmen in 50 major cities; NAB plans to add 75 more.

JOIN — *Job Orientation In Neighborhoods* — A government agency at the local level designed to recruit and train the

disadvantaged and serve as a feeder program for jobs. It has been
superseded in some communities by NMSC.

NMSC – *Neighborhood Manpower Service Centers* – As a
successor to JOIN, it recruits and trains the underemployed and
the undereducated for jobs in industry.

Use Educational Institutions

Predominantly Negro high schools and colleges are a good
source. General Electric has distributed to schools thousands of
copies of a booklet, *50 Progress Reports*, giving case histories of
careers of 50 of its Negro employees from managers to factory
workers. It has served as a successful recruiting publication. In
addition, GE employees – black and white – make hundreds of
speeches each year on high school vocational days.

General Electric and other companies also find it rewarding to
include Negro colleges on their recruiting trips.

Make Personal Contacts With the Negro Community

The white personnel man for a West Coast electronics organization moved into the Watts area of Los Angeles for three months.
Besides turning up numerous likely job candidates, he made
several other discoveries which led him to revise the use and
evaluation of aptitude tests and to hire Negro recruiters to launch
a recruiting campaign within the black community.

When you recruit, explain the job requirements with special
care to avoid rejecting the Negro applicant for reasons *inexplicable*
to him. Keep your expectations realistic about black applicants.
Don't be prejudiced against them because their speech, clothes,
and manners are different from whites'.

Evaluate existing hiring standards for relevancy. Do you really
need a high school graduate for that production job? Does a
record of arrest for disorderly conduct necessarily mean the
applicant will not prove a good employee? Does the fact that an
unmarried woman has a child necessarily mean that she won't be a
good and loyal secretary?

Finally, use tests if you insist, but don't rely on them as the only measurement. Negroes often look on tests as devices to prove them disqualified. Even if that's not true, such an attitude can still adversely affect how they do on the test.

In addition to tests, rely on your interviewer's impressions, and insist on and check out all references from previous employers (if any), schools, church, and referral agencies. When you ask for references, emphasize that you will hire no one whose references turn out to be false.

Keeping Negroes Aboard

Many managers have two worries when it comes to keeping blacks on the payroll. On the one hand, they want a constructive environment to keep the blacks from drifting away. On the other, they are concerned about the social consequences if an economic shift forces layoffs. Most companies furlough production workers on the basis of seniority. This means that Negroes would have the lowest seniority in a recently integrated work force.

Fears about the consequences of layoff may be exaggerated. Where layoffs have threatened – in the auto and steel industries, for example – management ingenuity and planning have softened the blow on many of the newly hired. Instead of individual layoffs, management may opt for temporary plant closings, as in the case of Chrysler. Ford, U. S. Steel, and Inland Steel have used short work weeks to minimize the need for layoffs. Some new employees are exempt from layoff altogether, as long as they remain on training programs. Other new employees who have had to be furloughed seem heartened by the unexpected flow of layoff benefits and the prospect of recall when business picks up again. Many who have been laid off showed they had found their sea legs in the industrial environment by landing new jobs.

To deal with the other worry – to create and maintain a constructive environment for integration – managers find that the need for concern dissipates when they follow the suggestions already discussed. To summarize:

1. Prepare your work force, individually if necessary, for integration.

2. Prepare initially hired Negroes.

3. Prepare subsequently hired Negroes.

4. Desegregate all facilities.

5. Fire incompetent Negroes, but with care.

6. Have a program to advance Negroes — and communicate it.

7. Promote fairly.

8. Provide training.

So important is this last factor that the next two chapters are devoted to the subject.

5 How Industry Trains the Disadvantaged

Some 30 million people in the United States today — or more than 15 per cent of the population — are officially classified as poor, and of these a substantial number, especially members of minority groups, suffer from chronic unemployment. In the 20 largest metropolitan areas alone, according to the U.S. Department of Labor, well over 250,000 unemployed Negroes lack adequate education and work experience.

How can business train these people? Often the only way is to begin with basic reeducation, but this section is mostly concerned with vocational training.* Such training programs are of four general types — company-instituted, community-sponsored, Negro-initiated, and government-sponsored.

Company-Instituted Training

A company usually organizes its own program without government aid or without joining other companies in a mutual project when it has specific training needs not often needed or duplicated in other companies, when it is big enough to justify a private program, or when it wants to use training techniques not readily available in or advocated by other companies.

Emerson Electric Company, St. Louis, for example, uses closed circuit television to show clerical trainees their job operations in

---

* See Chapter 7 for a discussion of basic reeducation.

slow motion. Hoffmann-La Roche, Inc., also uses audiovisual aids to train clerks in its Newark, New Jersey, offices.

In Huntsville, Alabama, International Business Machines Corporation makes computer operators out of high school dropouts.

Xerox Corporation, Rochester, New York, has developed a 19-week training program for unemployed men, many of whom have police records, bad credit ratings, and spotty employment histories. The participants receive classroom instruction, informal counseling, orientation to basic industrial procedures, and guided work experience.

Preemployment training proves especially important for hardcore applicants. Without it, businesses usually experience disappointing results. Most companies have to rely on preemployment training by outside agencies, but a few are large enough to start their own. For example, Polaroid has established Inner City, Inc., to carry on training and manufacturing projects in the Roxbury ghetto of Boston. Inner City offers a paid working experience to unemployed people of the neighborhood. They will then qualify to move on to career jobs in existing Polaroid plants or with other companies in the Boston metropolitan area. Inner City is financed entirely by Polaroid.

Sharing the training problems by forming a consortium is one plan that has spread. The group picks a member company or an outside consultant to handle the prejob work and even the on-the-job counseling. Arrangements have been made in such cities as St. Louis, Milwaukee, Cleveland, Minneapolis, and Kansas City. Lockheed has begun two training courses in the San Francisco area where more than 400 hard-core people will be trained for 40 companies in a consortium.

The McGraw-Hill Project

To learn how company-instituted training programs work, look at a modest project — that of McGraw-Hill Book Company, part of McGraw-Hill, Inc.

It seemed like the simple, direct thing to do — it just made sense.

That's how Edward E. Booher, book company chairman, describes his decision to sponsor a pilot project to train and hire 20 disadvantaged individuals. The firm put up $25,000 to finance the project. From such agencies as the Urban League, the Puerto Rican Community Development Project, Mobilization for Youth, and state employment services, it recruited twelve women and eight men, Negro and Puerto Rican, ages 18 to 44. Only a few had completed high school. Many had never held a job before, and even those that had were underemployed. Fifteen were assigned to New York City, five to the company's operation in Hightstown, New Jersey.

The problem of creating an entirely new program proved more difficult than imagined. Libert Diaforli, pilot program director and head of the office training staff that tackled this problem, said:

> I first had to establish what disadvantaged meant, to go deeper into the problem.

Other snags appeared. How do you instruct a person who has probably met with defeat through most of his schooling? Mr. Diaforli said:

> The solution was to divorce the classroom from the student, and still keep the student in his seat.

Fortunately, McGraw-Hill had already developed a communication-skills program which proved ideal for this purpose, and it formed the core of the supportive education that the group of 20 received over an eight-week period. Other McGraw-Hill educational materials were also extensively used to teach business math and English, typewriting skills, and other subjects.

For the men, there was less emphasis on clerical skills and more stress on on-job training, especially after the first six weeks of the course.

"We had to maintain a high peak of motivation," Mr. Diaforli pointed out. This was done by letting the trainees feel that they were genuinely participating and that they had a stake in the program. The trainees talked about their problems, interests, goals, and hopes.

Participation reached its peak during the general discussions held twice a week. These sessions often features films and guest speakers. Films on such subjects as problem drinking, human reproduction, Negro history, and social sciences were shown and discussions followed. Guest speakers came in to discuss home economics, banking and finance, marriage, and careers.

High motivation was reinforced by paying the trainees. Their pride in accomplishment and desire to succeed was nurtured by the attentive counseling of specialists from the office training staff.

The essential approach of the pilot project was described by Mr. Diaforli in this way: "Show you do care and show what McGraw-Hill can do for them. Show there is a place for them in society, that they can stand on their own."

Apparently this approach worked. Though no one insisted, many trainees came to class before 9 A.M. Many also preferred to work in class rather than to take their full lunch hour. Attendance was exemplary.

Did the pilot project succeed? The figures tell the story. Of 20 who started, 19 have been permanently placed in jobs ranging from clerk typist to billing clerk.

The McDonnell Douglas Project

A larger project was established in St. Louis by the McDonnell Douglas Corporation, maker of the famed Phantom fighter and prime contractor for the Mercury and Gemini space capsules. The reason for the project: a manpower shortage. McDonnell employs roughly 40,000 in its St. Louis plant; about half of them are production workers.

The company began hiring and training the disadvantaged several years ago. Because the aircraft and aerospace industry has become highly professionalized and technologically sophisticated, the decision to integrate into the work force individuals with little or no mechanical or mathematical background presented problems. Few products are more complicated and more dependent on accuracy and precise workmanship than the Phantom plane and the Mercury space capsule.

Thus, McDonnel faced a key question:

> How can a training program be established that would enable even a disadvantaged person with no previous experience to develop a basic skill within a relatively short time?

The company developed a four-month training program as a solution to this critical matter. First, for four weeks, the trainee spends several hours each day in classwork and more time on practice benches learning to drill and rivet sheet metal projects of increasing complexity. During the next 13 weeks, he moves onto the production line as a helper.

The trainee is paid during these four months, but the net cost to McDonnell is less than the out-of-pocket figure, $1,460, because the trainee performs useful work some of the time. Applicants must be basically literate, possess an eighth-grade grasp of arithmetic, and feel motivated to learn and work.

How well does the program work? Before initiating it, McDonnell experienced high turnover; now it enjoys a turnover rate in production jobs of 30 per cent a year, slightly lower than the industry average of 3 per cent a month.

Cooperating with Community-Sponsored Programs

Community-sponsored programs abound. Timken Roller Bearing Company undertook to ferret out all of them in its home city of Canton, Ohio (1960 population, 114,000) and uncovered 11, some of which even vocational guidance counselors in the area didn't know existed.

Many community-sponsored programs combine job-hunting and applicant-finding efforts with the training — a combination that makes sense because the best training project in the world won't be effective unless you can find a person willing to be trained and a job waiting for him once he has completed his course.

Work Opportunities Unlimited

One such combination program, founded in the fall of 1966, is
Work Opportunities Unlimited (WOU), brainchild of K. Brooks
Bernhardt, a personnel director of Monsanto Company in St.
Louis. The Department of Labor's Bureau of Apprenticeship
Training and the Office of Economic Opportunity provide most of
the funds for Work Opportunities Unlimited. Private local sources
provide the 10 per cent matching funds necessary for the federal
grant.

Besides ferreting out job applicants and the work for them,
Work Opportunities Unlimited also conducts on-the-job training
programs funded through the Bureau of Apprenticeship Training.
Under these contracts, employers select and train workers. The
employer is reimbursed up to $25 weekly for as many as 26 weeks
for training the potential employee. The men are trained as
welders, repairmen, assemblers, sales and accounting clerks, and
data processing operators.

Alfonso J. Cervantes, mayor of St. Louis, says:

> WOU is one of the first broad attempts in the nation by the business
> community to become involved in the crisis of the central city.

Aim-Jobs

Like WOU in St. Louis, AIM-JOBS in Cleveland also finds the
employers' basic work needs and then seeks participants who are
able to meet those needs. But AIM-JOBS is unlike some other
programs with the same goals: industry's contribution is two-fold.
Industry supplies the jobs and also *loans* executives to AIM-JOBS
to help coordinate and supervise the program — a large factor in its
success. The program is financed privately and through funds from
the Manpower Development Training and Economic Opportunities
Acts.

Participants recruited by AIM-JOBS from high-unemployment
neighborhoods take aptitude and skills tests and are given a
two-week orientation course at the AIM-JOBS Center in downtown Cleveland. The course includes discussions of proper ways to

apply for a job, attitudes, work habits, job performance, hygiene and grooming, getting along with other employees, and money management.

Money management starts at once with the presentation of $10 to cover the trainee's first week of transportation and lunches. Cleveland center officials report that one applicant in ten takes off with the money, but three out of four of those return and resume their orientation.

Once an applicant is on the job, he works closely with a coach or counselor who smooths the transition to the job.

Jobs Now, Inc.

Another successful program is Jobs Now, Inc., which operates in several cities, including Louisville, Kentucky. Jobs Now works with government, business, and private agencies who refer hard-core unemployed individuals to the Jobs center. There, they are assigned to a coach and participate in a two-week orientation program. This covers 29 basic areas, including application forms, pay checks, unions, hygiene, company work rules, budgeting pay checks, transportation, etc.

During the two weeks of the orientation program and for the first two weeks on the job, Jobs Now supports the client with an expense allowance for food and transportation. At the end of orientation, the man is matched with an available job which has been previously pledged by the participating companies.

A coach is then assigned to each man to assist him through one year of employment. The coach, an employee of Jobs Now, lives in the client's neighborhood, has had work experience, and has the ability to relate with the client as well as with the employer. The coach works closely with both the employer and the client to develop the necessary rapport to keep the man on the job.

Teenage Employment Skills Training

A somewhat special community program is Teenage Employment Skills Training (TEST), a Cambridge, Massachusetts, project supported through private contributions from foundations, businesses, and individuals. In addition, Cambridge businesses, including New England Telephone & Telegraph Company, Polaroid Corporation, and Broadway Super Market provide instructors for skill-training and trade-exposure programs. TEST receives no federal money directly, but counselors are paid in part from College Work-Study Program funds.

TEST helps Cambridge youngsters earn money, stay in school, and aim at either post high-school studies or skilled occupations.

TEST counselors are college students from Harvard, Radcliffe, Boston University, Boston College, and the University of Massachusetts. They come from the same kind of background as the enrollees and can understand and help them deal with their problems.

Because the counselors have "made it" – broken out of the cycle of poverty by obtaining an education – they are excellent models for these young people.

Work experience is central to TEST activities. Paid work, whether part-time or casual, puts money in the teenager's pocket and gives him a sense of independence. Then he is ready to think about staying in school or developing an occupational interest.

Before being referred to a job, each enrollee attends an employability course to learn proper methods of job application and on-the-job conduct. Informal classroom instruction and mock interview situations give him an introduction to the employer's expectations and provide insight into his own ability to meet them. In addition, a variety of skill courses are given to increase the enrollee's chances of obtaining a job.

The most important aspect of TEST counseling is that the enrollee is not coddled or given a handout. When the teenager is placed in a job or educational program, TEST stands behind him if he encounters problems and falters. The major responsibility, however, remains his own.

Cooperating with Negro-initiated Training

Opportunities Industrialization Centers

In 1964 an abandoned Philadelphia police station was converted into a job training center by a Negro minister, Rev. Leon Sullivan, who worked with industry to develop its financial and equipment support and the curriculum.

Since then, the idea of teaching young people in Negro and other minority groups the connection between earning and learning has grown to include some 70 cities where centers are located. Now called Opportunities Industrialization Centers, OIC receives and uses advice on curriculum from the businesses which hire its graduates. Businessmen supply some of the teaching and much of the equipment used in the training. Courses run the gamut of industrial, office, and commercial skills — all tailored to the needs of the potential employers.

The key to the program is that trainees acquire more than skills. They are also instilled with good work habits and pride in themselves, says the Rev. Mr. Sullivan.

OIC has also established satellite centers, such as the Antonini facility, named after a Puerto Rican leader in Philadelphia. The OIC slogan is, "We help ourselves." The Rev. Mr. Sullivan says a change in attitude is the first requisite. The unemployed or underemployed must develop a belief in his innate self-sufficiency and potential for progress. Appropriate motivational training is conducted at the Antonini Center, along with basic communication and mathematical instruction. Then the OIC candidate is ready for job training at another OIC location.

Career Development Center

Another example of Negro-initiated training is the Career Development Center in Detroit. Financed largely by white businessmen, it grew out of a black action group, the People's Community Civic League. The league was founded in 1956 by Alvin W. Bush as a means by which ghetto residents could help themselves. Initially, the group held barbecues and other fund-raising events to send black youngsters to summer camps or summer schools.

In 1957, members began to have doubts about this approach and started placing Negroes in jobs. But they made the same discovery as did the Rev. Mr. Sullivan; they had more trouble finding qualified people for jobs than in locating the work.

Out of this grew the Career Development Center which offers general educational courses to high school graduates and dropouts who have progressed at least through the eighth grade. In the planning stage are courses in welding, auto mechanics, electric appliance and equipment maintenance, cooking, and serving. No graded classes exist. Tests indicate a student's level of learning. Those who enroll pay $25, either upon entering, or from income after they get a job. Although the center was far from the target in 1968, it has a goal of 3,000 graduates a year.

Western Electric

In another approach to training cooperation with minority groups, Western Electric Company works with the Joint Apprenticeship Program of the Workers Defense League and A. Philip Randolph Foundation which prepares Negroes, Puerto Ricans and others for apprenticeship examinations in the building-trades unions. Western Electric volunteers conduct mock interviews in Harlem for men who have passed the examinations and who must appear for an oral screening before an industry-union committee.

The Western Electric volunteers assume the role of *the hostile white boss* or a member of the screening committee in face-to-face practice interviews to help potential applicants develop confidence and poise.

From the time the tutoring program started in 1965 until 1968, the number of Western Electric volunteers grew from 43 to more than 100. Over 300 young men, ages 18 to 25, from minority-group backgrounds have been placed in union apprenticeship programs for training as sheet metal workers, machinists, electricians, bricklayers, and in other trades.

Part of the success of the program lies in the businesslike approach of the Western Electric tutors. One volunteer, an information systems engineer, emphasizes that in relations with trainees he is "straightforward, blunt, frank, and not goody-goody. When necessary, I tell them I think they can do a lot better. I think they appreciate this. They're smart enough to know when people are talking just to please them."

Cooperating with Government Programs

Government programs proliferate – federal, state, and local. State and local poverty and employment agencies can help steer you through the maze, but if your company is located in one of the 50 largest cities in the U.S. (eventually in one of the 125 largest), you can get help from the National Alliance of Business-men (NAB).

On January 23, 1968, President Johnson issued an urgent call for a new partnership between the government and private industry to hire and train the hard-core unemployed. The President asked for a program to put 100,000 men and women on the job by June, 1969 and 500,000 by June, 1971 (President Nixon later increased the goal to 614,000). The National Alliance of Businessmen came into being to handle the business side of the Job Opportunities in the Business Sector program (JOBS).

NAB is a nationwide blue-ribbon panel of corporate executives. The officials come from 49 mainland cities and Honolulu. Each heads a local Alliance of Businessmen which handles the programs. The country is divided into eight regions with a chairman for each. There is also a headquarters in Washington.

The 50 cities each have one man with NAB who heads a local effort manned by home-town executive talent. Local groups are chartered as nonprofit corporations. In Chicago, for example, there is a board of 19 executives who represent the area's business and industry. This board, in turn, draws its working staff from local companies.

The federal government has funds available to pay the extra costs of training which employers may have to face when they take on the hard-core jobless. These funds are in addition to those which have been available under previously established projects, such as the Manpower Development and Training Act programs.

The alliance program draws on all established agencies which can assist in finding the jobless, training them, and helping them to make all the adjustments necessary to become productive and self-reliant. NAB does not by-pass local agencies, but often uses them as com-munication and referral centers. The alliance seeks to bind effec-tively through one agency all the community resources available.

Participating companies pledge that they will hire and train a specific number of people during the JOBS campaign period. The employer doesn't have to do all the training necessary if he lacks the facilities. The alliance can help to arrange training in any of the area's social agencies which may be equipped to do the job.

Or if the employer wants to do the training, NAB can help him get federal funds which will cover the extra costs of training needed to make the recruits employable, according to the employer's standards. (The alliance can also help with the paperwork involved in getting federal funds for this purpose.)

Then too, if it isn't practical for an employer to set up a federally funded training program on his own, he can join a group of employers by making an arrangement with the alliance. In this case, NAB sets up the training project and applies for the training funds. This government-supported training can also be handled by commercial schools or training operations. For example, Manpower Teaching Services, Inc., a division of the temporary-help agency, Manpower, Inc., has set up arrangements in many cities to provide various kinds of training.

But you don't have to accept federal funds to participate. Many companies handle the full costs of training. Nor do you have to take in anybody in the JOBS program. In all cases, the company makes the decision to hire or not to hire.

As of mid-1968, the Department of Labor had approved 428 projects to train more than 42,500 individuals. The government was prepared to pay out $350 million in 1968 for that year's programs. In addition to that, employers running the training classes also paid out millions for on-the-job training. The government money went for expenses of recruiting the disadvantaged persons, giving remedial education where needed, counseling and other special services.

Size of the classes ranges from one trainee in small businesses up to three thousand. Costs of the courses also vary widely, depending on the type and length of training needed. Some courses run 52 weeks; others only a few weeks.

One Pittsburgh project, to train for skilled jobs in construction, calls for an average government cost of $5,500 for each trainee. After 52 weeks, one man is to get a job as a pile driver, at $5.54 an hour. Another who finishes is promised $5.50 an hour as a carpenter.

Other projects will cost, generally, $2,000 to $3,000 for each worker. A low figure of $153 for each trainee was estimated for a Ford project at its Chicago Heights stamping plant. Production workers after four weeks in class were promised jobs paying $135 a week or $3.36 an hour.

We have now seen many examples of what businessmen can do to train disadvantaged youngsters. In the next chapter some of the ground rules that can help you perform this task more effectively will be considered.

6 Making Training Pay Off

Alexander N. McFarlane, board chairman for CPC International, Inc. (formerly Corn Products Company), says:

> The factory of the future will have to become a most effective instrument for education in our industrial society if it is to satisfy the needs of consumers and the higher ambitions of employees.

A study by Seymour L. Wolfbein, commissioned by the Chamber of Commerce of the U.S., *The Emerging Labor Force of the U.S.,* presents data concerning the major bridge which brings labor demand and labor supply together in this country — education, which also has served as the pathway toward upward social and economic mobility.

Table 6-1 shows the relationship between education and poverty in the mid-1960's. The same holds true for the relationship between educational attainment and unemployment. As recent data indicate, the jobless rate among those who do not finish high school is about double that of high-school graduates who, in turn, have a rate of unemployment almost triple that of college graduates.

The nonwhite has fared relatively poorly in the educational sweepstakes. As late as 1966, the median years of schooling among white workers 18 years of age and over was 12.3 (more than a high

Table 6-1

The Relationship between Education and Poverty in the 1960's

Education of Head of Family	Poverty Incidence
Total	19%
Less than 8 years of school	44
8 years	25
8-11 years	18
12 years	10
13-15 years	9
16 or more years	5

school graduation); for the nonwhite counterpart, the figure was 10.5, only a little beyond the sophomore year in high school. Yet, the nonwhite has a higher educational attainment than the white in the professional and clerical occupations (he often needs that extra to land this kind of job); but he falls badly behind in the other job fields.

The white-collar occupations have moved ahead of the blue-collar occupations and are scheduled for still further substantial increases in employment. (See Table 6-2.)

Dr. Wolfbein makes these predictions:

• Just about one of every two people who work will be a white-collar worker by 1975.

• One of every seven workers will be a professional.

• In fact, professional personnel will for the first time in our history outnumber the skilled craftsmen, the historic symbols of American industrial enterprise.

• Less than 5 per cent of all workers will be unskilled.

Unless disadvantaged people receive training, their plight will become worse, not better, in the years ahead because the uneducated person already has a much harder time finding a job than his better-educated counterpart and because the education demands are growing in the years ahead for business and industrial jobs.

Table 6-2

Change in Employment Groups

Occupational Group	Change for 1965-1975
Total	22%
White-Collar Total	33
Professional, technical	45
Proprietary, managerial	25
Clerical	31
Sales	23
Blue-Collar Total	14
Skilled craftsmen	24
Semiskilled operatives	12
Unskilled laborers	- 3
Service	35
Farm	-18

Guidelines for an Effective Reeducation Program

What guidelines can help businessmen make the factory and office effective instruments for education? From the case studies in the previous chapter and from other brief examples, the following guidelines can be developed.

Sell Supervisors and Other Management People on the Program

The Big 3 auto companies began a program in 1968 to hire the *unemployables*. Major difficulties arose with some management people, not with those hired. The auto companies acknowledge that attitudes among lower management men occasionally needed revision.

A Ford Motor Company official, briefing recruiters, was asked by one, "How do you know a guy with an African hairdo isn't going to blow up the plant?" A Negro consultant replied, "Do you think that every girl you see in a miniskirt is promiscuous?"

Moral: Persuade the people who will be running the program of its need and merits before you do anything else.

Sell Hourly and Clerical Employees on the Program

Edward W. Chave, second vice president for Equitable Life Assurance Society, emphasizes that hiring the disadvantaged poses problems to other employees, particularly those in personnel and operational functions. Those working with and around the hard-core people should be trained, sensitized, and given counseling.

Point out to all present employees — hourly, clerical, supervisory, and managerial — that they may serve as new models for the trainees. The typical ghetto recruit either has no parents or they are separated. His high-school teachers have obviously not served him successfully as models. On the job, his peers and his supervisor can serve.

Accept Different Standards of Efficiency during Training

Dr. Myron Woolman, a psychologist, notes that it is essential to deal with the trainees' existing values, rather than to attempt to sell them on *white values*. Dr. Woolman asserts that the greatest barrier to their successful employment is their totally humanistic outlook. Rather than thinking in terms of efficiency, schedules, and results, they think in terms of how they can get the money to buy a car or whether they are being accepted or rejected by fellow employees.

Dr. Woolman uses role-playing sessions which subtly suggest that trainees can get the things they want by learning to "make it in the white man's world" while maintaining integrity as a member of a minority group.

Role-playing sessions, termed the Losing Game and the Winning Game, have helped disadvantaged Negroes and other hard-core unemployed persons to adjust to the working-world environment. Dr. Woolman has used the approach in employment-preparation ventures at three Northern Systems Company plants and at the Lincoln Job Corps Center in Nebraska. He reports that 70 per cent completed training, and 90 per cent of those completing the program were still employed three months after completion.

Part of a factory-simulation program averaging 12 weeks for each trainee, the *game* approach was used one hour each day as simulated factory conditions gradually intensified in pressure. During the sessions, trainees were asked to act out scripts showing how employees became *losers* in handling on-the-job conflicts. Then they were asked to approach the same situations without scripts and come out *winners*. Group leaders, picked from the ranks of advanced trainees as the program progressed, asked questions provoking alternative ideas.

While you should accept different standards of efficiency during training, you should not give the disadvantaged special *dispensation* once they have completed their training, most (but not all) training specialists agree. Theodore B. Bloom, personnel director at a General Motors plant which employed the unemployables (ex-convicts, heavy drinkers, etc.) for the first time in 1968, says:

> Their performance on the job is at least equal to that of the regular employees.

Teach, if Necessary, the "4 R's" in Addition to Normal Job Skills

William A. Spartin, general supervisor of employment and recruitment for International Harvester says that Harvester gives four weeks of prejob training, completely isolated from the rest of the work force before offering eight weeks of training on the job. The company provides basic education and environmental training in the four-week period.

Dennis Derryck suggests a "4th R" — attitudinal readiness — in addition to training often found necessary in reading, writing, and arithmetic. As assistant director of the Joint Apprenticeship Program for the Workers' Defense League, he sees the need for attitudinal readiness that will commit the trainee to play by white rules and to maneuver within them. Then the trainee will come to realize that the 3 R's will help him to achieve whatever he wishes.

Use Visual Aids and Other Devices To Simplify Training

Design the program in small units, with each successive step reinforcing what has previously been learned. Make all aspects of the training relate as closely to the job as possible. If you teach reading, for example, relate the reading to the job. But because reading proves laborious for most disadvantaged people, stick to visual aids and other devices to simplify training as much as possible.

Many companies have found programmed learning effective. E.I. du Pont de Nemours & Company, for instance, created such a program for its own staff members, then adapted it for other purposes. Du Pont has invested about $3 million in the approach since its introduction in 1960.

Du Pont has supplied more than 100 programmed-instruction courses to nearly 1,500 firms, government agencies, and trade schools. Among the users is the Federal Reformatory at Petersburg, Virginia. Prisoners study industrial skills such as welding and automotive mechanics, as well as mathematics, accounting, and other subjects. (In programmed instruction, an area of knowledge is carefully broken into very small pieces of information which are presented to the student by a sequenced question-and-answer technique.)

Du Pont's program meets the needs of inmates especially well because they can work on one course at a time and at their own pace. They do not have to stand around while someone else works, a common complaint under more traditional forms of vocational training.

Dr. Garland S. Wollard, director of education for the Federal Bureau of Prisons, says the men at the Petersburg Reformatory do not feel they are being "used" by the institution when they take programmed instruction. They like the idea of learning by a system that "is good enough for a large corporation." Dr. Wollard plans to introduce the Du Pont system to the five other federal reformatories and two federal penitentiaries.

Records for about 70 inmates who have completed 177 courses show average marks of 90 per cent on final exams, and the men completed the work in much less time than under conventional instruction.

Use Tested Teaching Methods but in a Nonschool Atmosphere

You can train the disadvantaged most effectively in an environment as different from the schoolroom as possible. Keep classes small and informal. Use tables instead of the traditional desks. Have the instructor look and act as little like a conventional teacher as possible. Some companies use titles such as *advisor* or *trainer,* in an attempt to depart still further from traditional patterns.

For most disadvantaged people, the conventional classroom tends to evoke memories of past failures. Robert A. Graney, director of industrial relations at Inland Steel Company, says Inland finds that many youngsters leave school because they don't like the school situation, not necessarily because of failing marks. They do not want the feeling of being handled by social scientists, clerics, teachers — anyone who projects the image of "do gooder."

Paul W. Briggs, superintendent of Cleveland's public schools, says it's necessary to change the establishment to overcome the prejudice the hard-core people have against the educational system. In a work-study plant in Cleveland (see Chapter 7), the head man isn't called a *principal* but a *manager.* And some of Dr. Briggs' staff are dropouts themselves. Businessmen do part of the teaching.

Although you strive for a nonschool environment and although you emphasize visual aids and programmed learning more than conventional teaching does, training the disadvantaged still requires many of the traditional instructional techniques, such as these:

• Start with what the learner already knows, to give him confidence.

• Proceed slowly, bit by bit.

• Repeat, and repeat again, but in varying ways to avoid boredom.

• Insist on practice, especially in manual operations.

- Stimulate questions.
- Be encouraging.
- Show how the trainee will fit into the overall production or office pattern.
- Show how and why the work to be performed is needed and used.
- Put the learners on their own, at the right time, by asking them when they feel confident to "solo."

Be Patient, Sympathetic, but Firm

Teachers must establish contact, project empathy and compassion, advises Dr. Briggs. When they do, the student improves noticeably from the first day. Within three days, it becomes obvious whether the teacher will succeed.

Cleo W. Blackburn, executive director of the Board for Fundamental Education, says a teacher of the hard-core must relate to people rather than to subject matter. Students must be able to identify with him and realize that he is the solution to their problem. The teacher must begin at the level where the students *are,* rather than where he *wishes* they were. Mr. Blackburn says:

> The best teacher for a high-school dropout is a college dropout — provided he didn't drop out of a teachers' college.

An Eastman Kodak Company instructor, Frank Palmisano, explains why his company decided to take a firmer attitude toward absenteeism and tardiness in training classes:

> We checked on former trainees and found that those with poor attendance records in training did no better on the job. So now we deal with absenteeism in training — ask the problem cases what's wrong and how we can help them. If they still goof up in spite of our efforts, disciplinary action is taken.

Jack B. McCown, vice president of Firemen's Fund American Insurance in San Francisco, lets supervisors "spoon feed" trainees for a while. But he makes it clear   that he expects standards to be met on attendance and behavior.

Communicate Effectively with Trainees

Training people have discovered that they need to learn a new language when dealing with the disadvantaged.

When a trainee excused his tardiness with the explanation, "My hog was stolen," the supervisor's first inclination was to fire the boy for so impudent an explanation. But deeper probing revealed a translation: The finance company had repossessed the used car the trainee had purchased on time in a moment of euphoria when he had been hired. He had miscalculated his timing when forced to resort to public transportation.

Because many workers are reluctant to admit when they don't understand, verbal confusions crop up. A newly hired Puerto Rican clerk at a Bridgeport, Connecticut, company wanted to quit because she was "bored." Her exasperated supervisor almost let her go until he found that she really meant she was perplexed.

An instructor for an airframe manufacturer anticipates poor understanding by a daily check of his material for "suspect words." Then he writes them on the blackboard, with definitions, before the training period begins.

Some companies have assembled glossaries of ghetto words and phrases for use with their employees. Samples: A *blood* is a Negro; a *handkerchief head* is an Uncle Tom; *Mother's Day* is the first and fifteenth of every month when a woman can get state aid; a *bodiddley* is a down-home singer; a *hully gully* is a participant in the Watts riots; a *gas head* is a person who has a *process* or who takes drugs.

Peter G. Kontos of Educational Dimensions, Inc., Cleveland, points out another aspect of the communication problem:

> Research tells us that the incessant noise of the ghetto has conditioned many residents to ignore all sounds. Important instructions or orders may be unconsciously tuned out as more noise. The hard-core employee who seems to be pretending not to hear you or not to understand may not be acting. Much of the time he really didn't hear, or your directions just went over his head.

But even if you use the language of the ghetto, make allowances for *attitudinal deafness,* and employ the best mechanics and techniques of teaching, you will fail if you have inadequate empathy in your training. As you teach, ask yourself these questions:

- Am I presenting this clearly?
- Am I doing it in a way that I would have liked it presented to me?
- Do I believe in what I teach?
- Have I remained calm?
- Have I shown patience?
- Have I shown enthusiasm for the job and the company?
- Have I encouraged the trainee to higher performance?
- Have I corrected his mistakes tactfully, yet definitely?
- Have I praised generously and sincerely?
- Have I encouraged questions and comments?
- Have I made clear the standards of performance expected?
- Have I indicated the why, as well as the what, of the job?
- Have I made clear the rewards that come with a job well done?
- Have I made clear that the job carries with it the freedom to fail, provided that the failure is through ignorance and human error and not through willfulness or criminal carelessness?

The last point — freedom to fail — usually proves the most important to communicate to a trainee from a minority group. He probably expects to fail because he has lived with failure all his life. So vital is it for you to help break the vicious circle of failure that this area needs a special guideline.

Develop the Trainee's Pride

The trainee's failures probably long ago undermined his pride. He has had to make do with ersatz substitutes — belligerence, defiance, senseless insubordination, sullenness, and in extreme cases alcohol and drugs.

Motivation ends with failure, but it starts with pride. One good way to cultivate pride is to pay adequately while the hard-core person trains. This instills in him a sense of controlling and directing his own life.

Eugene Cox of Whittaker Corporation says that you motivate people powerfully when you show them how they can win tangible rewards.

> The best way to change attitudes about their future is to show them what they can get if they apply themselves.

Frank Libby, vocational training supervisor at Kodak, says,

> I try to get them addicted to the paycheck.

And Frank S. Jabes, an employee relations executive at TRW, Inc., adds:

> If you want to see some really motivated people, take a look at a guy who is having his first chance to make a living wage. You couldn't have a better employee.

International Harvester gives diplomas to trainees when they graduate to regular jobs. Mr. Spartin reports that more than one has responded by saying, "This is the first time in my life I ever got anything for finishing something."

You can develop the trainee's pride through many small, everyday actions. Examples:

• Praise when the praise is merited. And give the praise in the hearing of others.

• Censure when criticism is deserved, but do it in private.

• Keep your temper no matter how severe the provocation to lose it.

• Administer even-handed justice. You undermine the pride of others when you overlook transgressions of one trainee in the mistaken belief that such action won't be noticed by others or that it will somehow keep the peace. The minority member is especially sensitive to unjust punishment, seeing in it the pride-deadening kind of action he has experienced throughout much of his life.

• Treat the trainee as a human, not as a member of a minority group.

A 20-year-old dropout from the eighth grade echoes the sentiment of nearly all hard-core people: "I do want to become a man."

Provide a Job After the Training

Training must be for a job quite clearly in sight. Otherwise, few hard-core people will bother to take the training. Many have had bad experiences with earlier training, often government sponsored, which led nowhere.

And the work must be worthwhile. Negroes, ghetto blacks in particular, are sensitive to boredom, purposeless activity, and demeaning work – probably because they have already experienced so much of all three in their lives. The trainee will certainly expect the work to be boring, purposeless, or demeaning if the training is or if the instructor appears to consider it so.

Follow Up on the Trainee

Philco-Ford Corporation has a $1.45 million contract with the Department of Labor that, besides providing for the traditional counseling, prevocation training, and on-the-job training, has a unique recycling clause whereby a trainee who fails has a chance to repeat the six weeks at Philco when the instructors or the trainee himself can attempt to find out who or what went wrong.

Many job programs provide for follow-up because experience has shown that the *tender loving care* of the formal training period often needs to be continued for a while – especially in teaching the "4th R," attitudinal readiness. Some programs allow for as much as a year's follow-up by a special coach who lives in the employee's neighborhood and can counsel on personal problems.

Other programs aren't so elaborate. Perhaps they only involve use of the buddy system, with present employees providing continual coaching and moral support.

Dave Pope, former major league outfielder who is a coaching administrator for the AIM-Jobs project in Cleveland, says that if employers are patient and allow time and effort for follow-through, attitudes can change and productive, responsible employees will be the result.

Time and Cost of Training

Finally, we come to the core of the training problem: What will the extra time and effort cost? Of course, it depends on what you start with and the nature of the job for which you are training. The cost for each trainee can run from a few hundred dollars to several thousand.

On a modest level, IRC, Inc., a Philadelphia electronics firm, spends between $300 and $400 on each person; McDonnell-Douglas, $450 in St. Louis; Leon Sullivan's Opportunities Industrialization Centers report an average $900 for each trainee.

For more difficult cases and greater skills, the expense mounts. Lockheed-Georgia spends $700 of its own money plus $400 of government funds for each trainee. Humble Oil put out $1,200 for each man. Kaiser Engineering spent a total of $12,000 to train six draftsmen.

When you must cope with severely undertrained people, you may encounter heavy expenses. Robert Scanlon, training director at Whittaker Corporation, says his corporation's Instant Hiring program costs two or three times as much as conventional industrial training.

Are the extra training costs worth it? Norman Nicholson of Kaiser Industries speaks for many businessmen when he says:

> The costs of training are high. But riots and jails are also expensive.

Says the manager of a Philadelphia store that hired eight Philco-Ford trainees: "In the past we hired Negroes because we thought we had to. Now, we feel that these girls deserve to be hired on their own merits."

Isn't that the aim of every training program?

7 Can Industry Improve the Social Environment

At first thought, it would appear that business and industry should confine their efforts in facing the urban crisis to the areas of their principal competence — jobs and job training. Yet urban stability depends on more factors than jobs, and industry's competence encompasses a wider range of activities.

For the remainder of the book we will consider those areas not directly related to jobs, although all of them indirectly relate to work in the context that good jobs can't exist in a decaying society. As John W. Gardner, chairman of the Urban Coalition, puts it:

> Even today there are many in the universities and in the business world who somehow imagine that their special world can flourish while the society decays. It cannot be. Our society is wholly interdependent today, and decay in one part endangers all.

This section examines what business can do and is doing to arrest the dry rot in three areas — support of education, social services, and open housing.

Approaches to Educational Support

The Negro psychologist, Dr. Kenneth B. Clark, one of the directors of New York State's Urban Development Corporation, a

77

group set up to rebuild slums, especially relating to housing and schools, says:

> The most significant factor in urban instability is ... the social dynamite which is being produced by the criminal inefficiency of the inner city public schools. This is a matter directly related to the interests of business. First, a substantial proportion of the tax dollar paid by industry goes to support public schools. Second, the inner city public schools are producing human casualties which cannot be effectively integrated into the industrial and economic segment of our society unless additional funds are spent to compensate for the inefficiency of the public schools. In fact, business and industry are subsidizing inefficiency if they continue to permit public education to spawn hundreds of thousands of functional illiterates each year. Business and industry are caught in a double taxation bind if they are going to comply with equal employment demands of the federal government in other than token terms . . . . I suggest that business and industry take a leaf out of the history of the church and set up their own schools. Not vocational schools, not specifically industrial training schools, but schools starting from prekindergarten and going through the twelfth grade to demonstrate that the efficiency criteria, which seem to work so effectively in business and industry, can and will produce a more effective product than now being produced by the public schools.

Have businessmen gone as far as Dr. Clark suggests? Not many. But some are, knowingly or unknowingly, following some of his advice. Their programs fall into four principal areas – tutoring youngsters, offering remedial academic programs to employees, campaigning for better budgets and other administrative facets for the public schools, and introducing more realistic curricula – sometimes including radically new concepts – in the training of disadvantaged youth. Let's look at each more closely:

Tutoring Youngsters

The Quaker Oats Project. Employees of many companies now participate in programs to tutor youngsters in ghetto neighborhoods after school hours. In Chicago, 47 men and women with middle-class backgrounds – employees of the Quaker Oats

Company – are bussed once a week after working hours to a housing project where they tutor Negro children between the ages of 8 and 12. Each volunteer works for an hour and a half with two children who, in the opinion of their teachers, need special help in reading skills.

According to the Chicago Housing Authority, which oversees the tutoring, the children have been tripling their normal progress in reading skills. Six other companies in Chicago now participate in similar ghetto tutoring programs.

The Street Academy. A new type of project is the Street Academy program sponsored by the Urban League in New York, Newark, Paterson, and Trenton, New Jersey, to enable capable youngsters to qualify for college instead of dropping out of high school. Fifteen private corporations, as of December 1968, assumed sponsorship of a Street Academy.

Sponsorship entails a minimum one-year commitment to cover the operating expenses of a Street Academy, as well as the fix-up costs to convert a store front, garage, etc. Operating expenses include staff salaries, instructional materials, rent, light, heat, transportation, and telephone.

McGraw-Hill is one supporting corporation, its contribution on the order of $50,000 a year. From 9:00 A.M. until 3:30 P.M., closely following normal school hours, the McGraw-Hill facility admits some 30 students (40 to 45 are expected eventually). Late afternoon and evening tutorial classes are also planned. Subjects include math, English, sociology and the social sciences, science, and much remedial instruction for New York City youngsters.

Students regularly attending the McGraw-Hill Street Academy remain on the rolls of their high school, Haaren. The problems at Haaren typify the problems of ghetto education. Haaran is an academic high school, yet in June 1968 only one student received an academic diploma – the kind that qualifies for college admission. The others received the general diploma, worth little as a college admission card. It's like a general discharge from the Armed Forces – better than dishonorable, but less than honorable. Furthermore, of 2,300 students who started the school year at Haaren, only 1,500 will be around the following June.

Offering Remedial Academic Help to Employees

Many employers of disadvantaged people find that they must inaugurate training in academic subjects for at least two reasons:

- Employees who are functionally illiterate or who can read and write at only a low level of efficiency make ineffective employees.
- The offering of such training serves as a recruiting lure for many hard-core jobless.

Hotpoint High. General Electric's operation which makes the Hotpoint appliances is located in Chicago on the edge of a predominantly Negro area. Beginning in late 1963 when it started to build up its work force, it found that it no longer could attract the white suburbanites, its traditional labor pool. Where once Hotpoint employed almost no Negroes, now they make up nearly a third of its 3,600-employee hourly force. The number of Spanish-speaking employees of Puerto Rican and Mexican origin has increased from 400 to 700.

One approach with long-range potential is a program in which workers who haven't completed high school can attend in-plant classes on their own time and thereby upgrade their skills. The Chicago Board of Education provides the teachers for the classes and pays their salaries, while Hotpoint covers the costs of books and other school materials. Instruction is in reading, writing, arithmetic, spelling, social studies, and other subjects.

Hotpoint High is just one of many programs for disadvantaged employees hired by General Electric. Others include a course on credit understanding, a special induction program, an orientation arrangement, a counselor approach for special problems, and extensive skills training.

MIND, Inc. CPC International's subsidiary, MIND, Inc., in Greenwich, Connecticut, offers a private-enterprise answer to the question: How do you assimilate the unassimilables into the labor market?

MIND (derived from the words, Methods for Intellectual Development) offers a 160-hour course designed to improve the grade equivalency of the participants by about three levels. The concept of Charles F. Adams, who heads MIND, is to convince corporations of the need to upgrade low-level personnel, sell the companies the audio equipment and workbooks that go with the course, train monitors who can guide the course participants and supply the expertise required to get the in-plant program under way.

The cost to the companies, Mr. Adams says, works out to less than $400 for each trainee.

> In some labor markets, this makes training people cheaper than hiring new employees.

MIND, which aims to make a business of education, started as a development of that bastion of private enterprise, the National Association of Manufacturers. The association hired Mr. Adams in mid-1964 as an employee relations consultant to design a pilot system for developing human resources. The association invested more than $150,000 and the Stern Family Fund contributed $30,000 to initiate what was then called Project Mind.

In February, 1967, CPC International took over MIND (no actual sale was necessary), put in a large sum to capitalize its new subsidiary, and set up a headquarters employing 65 people. MIND had a respectable sales volume of $1.5 million in 1968 and expects even more in 1969.

The Equitable Program. In 1962, the Equitable Life Assurance Society began a program to hire high-school dropouts for some of its low-skill jobs. By 1966 it decided that it needed to add academic training. A counselor summed up the reason by saying, "A boy comes to us with either high hopes or a cynical attitude about the opportunity we are offering. The types of work initially assigned and the fact that the people they are competing with are better prepared for advancement dampens hope or renews cynicism."

The company therefore agreed to try to give the 1966-male-dropout group both a job and a "strong assist in improving their education." Equitable entered into an agreement with the Board for Fundamental Education — a nonprofit organization chartered by Congress to improve the education of those not prepared by prejob schooling for advanced work assignments. The board agreed to prepare the boys for the New York State high school equivalency examination and guaranteed success.

Eighteen boys started the 1966 program. Classes began the day they reported for the job and were held four nights a week, two hours a night. Thus, Equitable and the board took the risk of asking youngsters unwilling to continue formal schooling to work at a job all day and study for two hours at night. The boys, of course, were aware that they had to assume this load when they joined Equitable.

Of the 18 boys who started the program, 11 were still on the job at the end of May 1967. One had already won his diploma. Although the board estimated that the course would take 62 weeks, all but one of the others were ready to take the equivalency examination between June 1 and June 30, 1967 — bettering the original estimate by one-third. This record was especially remarkable because the 1966 turnover at Equitable among male employees of ages 16 to 19 reached an all-time high of 98 per cent.

Project Upgrade. Note that many of the programs combine academic with vocational training. Brunswick Corporation supervises a Chicago program, Project Upgrade, underwritten by a Manpower Development and Training Act grant which seeks to train 800 hard-core unemployed. Participants take a 30-week course covering reading and arithmetic, in addition to the specialized skills needed to enter job-training programs in the machining, fabrication, marketing, or service industries.

Joel Snyder, with Brunswick's Community Resources Division at the program's inception, reports that tactful, intelligently applied discipline can be effective.

> As a group, the hard-core hasn't had much success following the rules, and you'll gain more by explaining the why of safety rules, than by just laying them down and expecting compliance. Appeal to the worker's

pride by recognizing good work; make it clear that you'll only accept good work and you'll get what you want.

That holds for academic as well as vocational training.

Aiding the Schools

Business and industry can aid the public schools in many ways, including technological help. That facet of assistance is discussed in Chapter 11, but now let's touch upon mundane, but effective, approaches to aid through nontechnological means.

At General Electric's plant in Evendale (near Cincinnati), Ohio, nine employees are school board members. Here's a way business-men can directly influence public education. In some localities, school boards experience difficulty in persuading some citizens to run for a position on the body which directs the administrative and budgetary functions of most public school systems.

Comments one school board president: "We can get cranks and young lawyers wanting to make a start in their political careers to run, but we have much greater difficulty finding experienced businessmen willing to put themselves before the voters."

One Evendale GE employee who took the plunge is Calvin H. Conliffe, a project engineer at the jet-engine plant. In 1963, Mr. Conliffe became the first Negro to be elected to the Cincinnati Board of Education. In 1967 he was the only incumbent reelected to a four-year term. After his reelection, he was made vice chairman of the board. Mr. Conliffe has been especially active in programs whereby the schools and industry cooperate to persuade youngsters from disadvantaged areas to complete their education. The key argument: The best industrial jobs go to the best qualified people.

In Detroit, Michigan Bell Telephone Company has *adopted* Northern High School, and Chrysler has adopted Northwestern High. For both all-black schools, the sponsor company provides business experts to help revamp teaching techniques, and industry money goes for new equipment, to hire additional teachers, and to add more space for pupils.

Pittsburgh businessmen have allied themselves with educators and civil and religious groups to support a local, revamped educational system that includes replacing all the city high schools with five super high schools — to offer high-quality education in a racially integrated atmosphere.

On another level, the Chase Manhattan Bank Foundation has underwritten a Great Teachers program conducted in collaboration with the United Negro College Fund. Some of the nation's outstanding economics professors spend a week or two at many Negro colleges, lecturing, conducting seminars, and advising faculty members. General purpose: to stimulate interest in business among black students.

Introducing More Realistic Curricula

Businessmen can make significant contributions to the curricula and to the methods of teaching disadvantaged youth. For example, the Cleveland school system and area industries are cooperating in a new approach to the problem of school dropouts and unemployment with a program combining classroom work with on-the-job training. The project will be conducted in a four-story, former warehouse donated by General Electric. A $2 million grant from the President's JOBS program has implemented the project which began operations in 1969.

The former GE building, located in a ghetto area, will serve as a school-factory offering basic and remedial education, training in job skills, and paid work experience in business-sponsored work areas. (The Cleveland Board of Education will operate the school-factory.) The program will expose participants part of the day to an environment devoted to learning what it takes to get and hold a job, covering such subjects as basic reading, writing, and mathematics, as well as money management, personal hygiene, and good work habits.

The rest of the day participants will be assigned to work for on-the-job training. During this period, trainees will be paid by the participating companies for work performed while they learn their job skills.

After a training period geared to each individual's interest and capacity to learn (not to the traditional nine-month school year), the center will channel trainees into full-time employment.

Cleveland School Superintendent Paul W. Briggs points out that the unemployment rate in Cleveland's inner city is 15.5 per cent, the highest jobless rate of any inner city in the U.S. Even more significant is that, among the youths in the 17 to 25 age bracket who are no longer in school, 58 per cent are unemployed. By comparison, the Cleveland metropolitan area had an overall unemployment rate of less than 3 per cent in 1968.

Compounding the problem is an excessively high dropout rate from inner-city schools. About 4,000 students drop out of Cleveland schools each year.

Supplementing Social Services

One area where industry has shown imagination is in social services. Although such help has to be largely supplemental, there is a wide range in the types of assistance. Examples:

• In Cambridge, Massachusetts, KLH Research and Development Corporation has received a federal grant to help pay the cost of establishing a pilot program to provide an all-day, year-round school for young children whose fathers or mothers work in the nearby plant. The company has found that many employees were forced to quit, often to go on welfare, because they had no place to leave their children while they worked. Tuition for the school will be based on the employee's ability to pay.

• General Electric's Lamp Division joined with the city of East Cleveland, Ohio, to provide a summer day camp for under-privileged children in that municipality. Beginning in the summer of 1968, the company made available its Nela Camp recreational area, hitherto reserved principally for employees, for an eight-week day camp. Staffed and supervised by the city, the camp serves a total of 600 East Cleveland youngsters between the ages of 8 and 12.

Four two-week sessions, each to accommodate 150 children, were scheduled in 1968. The planned activities included nature studies, crafts, sports, swimming, and other camping activities. Nela Camp is a seven-acre recreational and conference area. Facilities include a swimming pool, wading pool, baseball diamond, auditorium, and play area.

• When a privately supported home for unwed mothers was on the verge of closing because of insufficient funds, a pharmaceutical firm rescued it financially, but its management advice probably proved even more beneficial in the long run. A company executive with experience in Red Feather campaigns headed a successful money-raising drive for it.

• Operation Bootstrap is an effort to win the cooperation of local Chicago gangs (or social groups as they are sometimes euphemistically referred to) in solving social problems. Organized in early 1967, the plan is backed by the police and industries such as Hotpoint, Sears Roebuck, Western Electric, Illinois Bell Telephone, and organizations such as the Urban League, the Chicago Commission on Human Relations, and the Board of Education, as well as neighborhood groups and religious leaders.

Divided into committees to get at the tougher problems facing them, the Bootstrap groups have: an employment unit dealing with such problems as the inability of young people with police records to get jobs; an education committee helping social and educational dropouts to get the training they need to qualify for jobs; a conservation and housing unit working on local urban renewal; and a social and recreational group providing constructive rather than destructive outlets for the gang members.

• But the most common, and probably the most efficient, way business and industry can contribute to social services is through United Community Funds — in terms of giving money, lending people to participate in local drives and to manage the local funds, and in selecting the projects to receive United Fund support.

The corporate share of total contributions to United Funds steadily declined from 38.3 per cent of the total in 1956 to 31.2 per cent in 1966; however, 1967 witnessed a leveling of this downward trend. Professionals in United Fund work project a steady increase in corporate giving both in the proportion of the total receipts and in the total dollar amounts from company contributions.

In fact, United Fund people say contributions of the order shown in Table 7-1 are necessary to keep pace with projected national economic growth.

Table 7-1

Minimum United Fund Contributions
Needed for the 1969-1975 Years

Campaign Year	Total Amount Raised (in millions of dollars)	Corporate Giving		Individual Giving	
		Amount	% of Total	Amount	% of Total
1969	$ 753	$234	31.1	$519	68.9
1971	846	265	31.3	581	68.7
1973	951	298	31.3	653	68.7
1975	1,060	335	31.6	725	68.4

To get an idea of the increase called for in corporate giving, compare the figures given in Table 7-1 with these amounts given by business and industry in the past: $153.8 million in corporate contributions in 1959; $174.8 million in 1963; $186.6 million in 1964.

The United Fund is often the ideal medium through which the smaller firm, particularly, can help supplement social services. (Chapter 15 contains a more detailed discussion of corporate giving.)

The Problem of Open Housing

In 1960 an urban white father of three had to earn at least $4,200 a year to afford standard housing, but a nonwhite father of three had to earn almost one-third more, or $5,500, to afford comparable quarters. The reason: Housing in most U.S. cities is still not truly open. Therefore, nonwhites have fewer units to choose from.

Discussion about what business can do and is doing to upgrade the physical standards of housing is deferred until Chapter 11. First, some comments on the environmental problem of open housing should be considered. Unfortunately, only scattered evidence turns up that business can do or is doing much in this area. Social pressures prove formidable, despite federal laws and statutes in many states and cities supporting open housing.

A national company admitted a civil-rights group's charges that it had no black people in management positions in its Southern plants. "We have been unable to recruit a single Negro qualified for a management job who is willing to live there," wrote the vice president of employee relations. He appeared to believe that such a comment settled the matter for good. Yet, some companies have tried to go further. They have supported community programs in such cities as Atlanta, Georgia, Huntsville, Alabama, and others and have helped toward desegregating services which, as much as housing, have been the major hurdle.

As an indication of the scope of the problem with housing itself, consider the experience of a group of Milwaukee home builders and apartment owners. Forty-five of the city's biggest placed half-page ads in the newspapers and in Negro weeklies. Addressed to Milwaukee's 26,000 Negro families, the ads pledged an unqualified "no segregation" policy in the sale or rental of housing.

Coming after months of turbulence over the open-housing issue — demonstrations were conducted for more than 200 consecutive days by the Rev. Mr. James E. Groppi, a Catholic priest, and his followers — the ads might have been expected to bring requests from Negroes for housing in what are now all-white areas of the city and its suburbs.

Not so. The response was disappointingly small. Ray A. Alexander, community relations director for an inner-city development council, explained:

> They [black people] don't believe the ads .... This statement of faith is commendable, but there hasn't been any action to alleviate some of the other problems.

He added that the basic need still hadn't been met for more low-cost housing.

But businessmen can point to some positive accomplishments:

• When Quaker Oats Company, which now operates some 35 plants throughout the country, decided to build a multimillion-dollar facility, it cast about for a suitable location. The community of Danville, Illinois, seemed promising, but it didn't have an open-housing law with teeth in it. Quaker Oats President Robert D. Stuart, Jr., indicated to the mayor that a meaningful ordinance would be favorably considered by the company. Putting such a matter on the line worked. Danville did pass such an ordinance four to one, and Quaker Oats promptly announced its intention to build there.

• When J. L. Hudson, the Detroit department store, led an open-housing fight in November, 1967, 10,000 customers closed their accounts. But Hudson persisted (and its business still flourishes).

• Many employees campaign for open housing on an individual basis. For instance, individual General Electric people have helped in Pittsfield and Springfield, Massachusetts; Lynchburg, Virginia; Schenectady, New York; Birmingham and Huntsville, Alabama; Cleveland; and Philadelphia.

Typical of these is Joseph P. Spampinato who worked with the Housing Association of Delaware Valley in Pennsylvania. The association operates on a regional basis in the eastern part of the state, helping to provide leadership to many community housing groups. Mr. Spampinato, who is a manager at GE's Valley Forge, Pennsylvania, Space Technology Center, has been active with the association since 1964 and is on the board of directors. He reports that association activities range all the way from "political pressure to helping individuals get fair treatment in trying to find housing." The association tries to assure that realtors and landlords live up to Pennsylvania's strong open-housing law, whose enactment the association contributed to.

New Corporate Approaches to the Social Environment

As a profit-making organization, what's a business' business in educating the uneducated, supplementing social services — all supposedly provided or guaranteed by government or private philanthropy — or fighting for open housing?

L. W. Moore, president of American Oil Company, gives this answer:

> Business and industry, in the normal conduct of their affairs, have long occupied a prominent role in the achievement of social progress. Our economic system, in fact, has created the abundance that has made most social progress possible .... But business, in turn, has benefited from the progress that has been made, and some of its own progress has been based on technological advances that are contributing to the problems that society faces today ... We need to sustain and enlarge the nation's economic progress, and our own, by involving ourselves with society and its problems in new and imaginative ways.

You can participate in many imaginative ways. Before delving into specific guidelines to help you determine your involvement in education, social services, and open housing, consider some general parameters.

Eleven Environmental Questions

1. Is any one individual responsible for facing the urban crisis in your company?

In medium and smaller companies, the president often functions as an *urban affairs manager*. In larger companies, an executive may be assigned the responsibility. In any event, somebody should be the focal point for urban matters — formally or informally designated.

2. Will your contribution in education, social services, and open housing provide a measurable corporate return?

Vague do-goodism won't help you, and it probably won't aid the cause significantly. It may even harm it. A midwestern office equipment manufacturer, in a spirit of public service, underwrote in the newspaper serving its community a series of ads urging open housing. The cause was not advanced when a subsequent letter to the editor pointed out that three top officials in the company lived in the area's most restricted suburb.

The corporate return may not result in dollars, but it should include benefits to employees and their families, a more favorable attitude by one of your key publics, or a better climate in which to pursue business objectives.

3. Can your company afford the investment in time, personnel, or money that will be required to make a significant contribution to the cause which interests you?

A common shortcoming in corporate efforts in these areas is to underestimate the resources needed. Sometimes, a businessman pulls out of a project when the full requirements become apparent, to the good of neither himself nor the cause.

In short, look before you leap. Survey the situation with care. Use your best business judgment to determine what's required. Make crystal clear to all concerned the extent of your commitment.

4. Can your company afford *not* to make the investment?

Warner & Swasey Company, machine tool manufacturer, entered into community action to protect its investment in its future in the inner city — on the edge of the predominantly Negro Hough area of Cleveland. Howard Geyer, vice president, says:

When relocation comes up in corporate planning sessions, we aren't altruistic. We've got too much at stake right here in the city. The high cost of relocation alone is as effective an anchor as you'll find anywhere.

So, when you consider costs of participation, factor into your analysis the costs of not getting involved. Frequently it proves higher than the expense of involvement. Besides relocation, weigh what inaction might cost you in terms of deteriorating quality, through poor education or health, of the labor pool from which you draw your potential employees.

5. Can other employers in your area share in the investment?

You are often in a better position to persuade another company to help out than representatives of civil-rights groups, school boards, or city governments. You can sell the idea effectively when you show that you have already bought it yourself. Warner & Swasey joined with other Cleveland companies in a housing effort, for example.

Joint projects offer many advantages: you share costs; you minimize danger of charges of paternalism; you spread the risk; you broaden the base for management consultation; you gain a broader commitment for success.

6. Is another employer better qualified than you to undertake a particular project?

American businessmen possess an immense and widely diversified range of talents. Somebody else may have the specific skills or experience needed when perhaps yours only approximate the requirements.

A Baltimore manufacturer seriously considered aiding a local high school to revamp the curriculum for a shop course. One of the manufacturer's managers discovered that another company in the city had already performed that task for the trade school in its area. In this case, the manufacturer needed only to adapt the other's course slightly for its high school's purposes.

Moral: Don't keep reinventing the wheel. In your appraisal of the situation, include a search to learn if other companies have dealt with similar problems earlier or have the expertise that can be readily adapted for the current challenge.

7. Can you sell the project to all your important management?

Here's a common stumbling block. The problem lies not so much with the vociferous objector. If he's important enough and his criticism sufficiently valid, he can probably stop your participation before it begins.

The silent objector is the man who usually performs the abortion in midpassage, often merely by dragging his feet. He's the fellow who "doesn't want to say anything" when the president announces the company's participation, but he has "had doubts all along about the wisdom of getting into this social-service business."

Spot the silent objector early. He has probably shown such delayed reactions before. Work on him with special care. A perceptive president assigned the major responsibility for a social-service project to a manager he suspected as a silent objector. As the manager grew more deeply involved in the project, he found himself emotionally committed. He made certain that it would succeed.

8. Can an employee or group of employees handle the project more effectively on an individual basis than you can on a company basis?

Some educational, social service, and open-housing matters often lend themselves better to individual than to corporate treatment. But the company must encourage the individuals to participate, publicly recognize their efforts, and perhaps even provide a reasonable amount of time off to pursue such activities.

Tutoring youngsters is an individual proposition. The extent of Quaker Oats' corporate involvement in the Chicago project, for example, is to recruit employees willing to participate and to provide transportation to and from the place of tutoring.

Corporations headquartered in large metropolitan areas. such as New York City, have found it much more practical and effective to quietly support their employees' efforts for open housing in the many geographically dispersed communities where they live than to issue broad exhortations.

Social-service work often involves individual counseling – in family problems, for example – which would be senseless to perform on a corporate basis.

You can tackle some environmental projects on both the corporate and the individual basis – in United Fund campaigns, for instance.

9. Does the project truly present a frontal attack on the urban crisis?

Corporate aid to the Boy Scouts is praiseworthy, but that organization is still largely middle and upper class (although it is beginning to try to change that). In this area, you would face the urban crisis head-on by supporting Boys Clubs, which work more directly with disadvantaged youths than does the Boy Scouts.

Corporate help to the school system of a wealthy New York suburb may make sense, but not in the context of the urban crisis. Here's a question of priorities. Business and industry can't do everything that needs doing. Perhaps the company that traditionally has aided the prosperous suburban hospital will have to shift its attention to the ramshackle one in Harlem.

10. Is your project primarily local in nature?

In general, business and industry experience the best results with local programs, not national or regional ones. Even the large companies such as Ford Motor find it best to work in the locations where their plants are or where their employees live. Then they have the local touch. They are more likely to possess intimate knowledge of the area. The employees who implement the program have greater personal commitment on local projects than they would on national ones.

Furthermore, problems involving these three matters normally vary widely from location to location. A national approach often would lack relevancy. Where national programs seem justified, you can usually leave them to government or the big foundations.

11. Do your projects give the disadvantaged the chance to help themselves?

Equitable Life avoids the dangers of paternalism in several ways. It assists ASPIRA, oriented to New York high school students of Puerto Rican background. Through its clubs, ASPIRA draws high school students into its organization with the aim of developing a committed Puerto Rican leadership. The clubs have cultural and educational programs and workshops, as well as social functions. Individualized counseling and tutorial aid are also provided, as well as financial help for those continuing to college. An understanding exists that, after college, the students will return to the community to help others.

Equitable was the first business to fund The Real Great Society, on Manhattan's Lower East Side. The young men and women in it established a University of the Streets, which provides tutorial help for students in the neighborhood. The group also babysits for mothers on welfare, who are thereby free to learn sewing skills in order to get jobs as seamstresses. In addition, the group has helped members who wanted to start a local business.

The insurance company is also developing a program with the National Medical Association, composed primarily of Negro physicians, to bring comprehensive health care to deprived sections of our cities and to stimulate talent recruitment, training, and employment of people in poverty areas.

Don't make your aid a handout; make it a handup. And you don't hand up by imposing assistance – no matter how well-meaning – from on high. Work through existing groups in the area. Use their ideas; don't impose yours. Give your assistance where the local groups lack resources – in money, management know-how, technical expertise, or equipment. The major drawback to government welfare is that it's little more than a handout.

The foregoing eleven questions can help you generally to focus your involvement. Next, consider specific aids to keeping you on the right track in educational, social-service, and open-housing programs.

Guidelines for Education

In your educational aid, the principal problem is to devise criteria that will measure progress and results. This usually proves relatively simple in tutoring youngsters or offering remedial academic help to employees. You can measure progress and results in the traditional pedagogic way — with exams. But how do you determine whether your aid to schools pays off? You can't know precisely, but with the following criteria you can approximately judge your impact:

Measuring Progress

Do the schools come to you for assistance or must you take the initiative? At the beginning, you probably must take the lead, but later a good sign of the effectiveness of your help appears when the schools approach you. Check to see if you receive annual invitations to participate in vocational days. If you have recruiting literature, learn whether the schools ask for it regularly or whether you have to press it upon the guidance counselors. Determine whether the counselors come to you concerning job requirements and related matters.

Keep track of the frequency with which you receive requests for special assistance — on curriculum, concerning equipment, on management matters, for technical advice. If the routine and special approaches are fairly frequent, indications are strong that you have a good payoff. If the approaches are rare, reappraise your situation.

Do students in the schools that you help apply for jobs at your company in significant numbers? If they do, are most of them well qualified for your jobs? If you can answer both questions affirmatively, you have a good indication of high payoff. If you must answer negatively to one or both, your performance, of course, appears less effective.

Do students themselves accept your aid with enthusiasm? Do they even know about it? You can judge the reaction yourself when you offer remedial academic help to employees.

A company that offered high school equivalency courses to disadvantaged employees on company property puzzled over the declining interest in the program which was run by the local board of education but paid for by the employer. The company learned that the employees didn't like the schoolroom atmosphere and the autocratic attitude of some of the instructors — the very factors which had led many of the employees to drop out of school originally. When the company changed these matters, enrollment immediately picked up.

But in aid rendered at the school itself, you will have to rely largely on the feedback of the school authorities. You can, however, discreetly inquire among the students themselves — at job interviews, for instance. If students aren't aware of your role, take steps for more recognition — from the educators, through publicity in the local newspapers. Or consider the possibility that the lack of recognition may stem from a more fundamental cause, the fact that your aid has not proved particularly noteworthy.

Is the dropout rate improving? Are more students going on for post high school study?

Is the teacher-student ratio improving?

Is the curriculum broader? Are the math, science, business, and shop courses up to date and competently taught?

Such criteria will do more than measure how you're doing; they will also help you to determine what to do by indicating shortcomings.

Knowing What To Do

Other questions to ask yourself in deciding what to do:

What is your company best qualified to do? Is it to give money, equipment, managerial know-how, technical expertise, or plain human support in counseling and tutoring? Perhaps you can offer a combination of all these, but in any event, decide on your tactical and strategic approaches, with your *urban affairs manager* participating in that decision and charged with implementing it.

What does your company need from the public school system? Besides providing a good source for employees, do the schools help upgrade human values and pride in self?

A midwestern company concerned about human values among youth in its area hired a retired professional athlete who had become a minister to spend five mornings a week counseling youngsters at the local high school.

Employees of a textile company volunteered to help coach baseball, basketball, and track teams at a predominantly Negro high school which previously had only the resources for a football squad. A lawyer for the same company organized and coached a debating team at the school, the first in its history.

What do the schools need from your company? When Equitable asked that question in the south Bronx of New York, it ended up helping to support the South Bronx Community Action Theatre, begun by two teachers, three parents, and 27 young people. The project now involves 16 teachers, 27 parents, and more than 300 youngsters.

How can you help to get more and better teachers (a chronic problem in any school no matter where it is)? When a small Southern high school lost its lone science teacher for 12 weeks because of illness, a paper mill in the area lent its chemist to teach his classes. That experience pointed up the need for more and better teachers, and the mill was instrumental in locating, and helping to support, a second science instructor for the next school year.

How can you get employees more involved in educational matters? General Electric encourages its people to do so by publicizing their efforts in the plant publications and by providing a reasonable amount of time off to pursue such activities. School board members in different GE plant locations compare notes from time to time and exchange ideas.

Is your help to education relevant? A pharmaceutical firm donated a new chemistry laboratory to a ghetto high school. A check at the end of the school year revealed that it had been little used.

Moral: Make your assistance pertinent. The pupils in this particular school were not yet ready for a sophisticated setup more suitable for second-year chemistry students in an affluent community.

Another common error: Too much aid goes for material things, not enough for human. While schools in disadvantaged areas sometimes lack facilities, they always need more of the human touch. This goes beyond the perennial need for more teachers. It involves providing for more coaching on scholastic, personal, and vocational matters. It involves organizing parents' associations or reviving moribund groups. It involves dissuading youngsters from quitting school, or it involves finding means whereby the bright ones can go on to college.

Getting Started

We come finally to a third general problem in making educational aid effective – how to get started. You might think that this is the problem to deal with first. Don't you first have to know how to get started before you know what to do and how to measure results? A major fallacy lies here. Many companies deal only with the question of getting started and never give enough thought to the subsequent matters. We leave it until last because you should consider it last.

Actually, getting started rarely proves very formidable. Begin with the top official responsible for the school or schools in the disadvantaged area which interests you. If he hasn't a list of needs as long as your arm, he's either incredibly lucky or incompetent. Match his needs as closely as possible with what you have already decided you are best equipped to offer.

Guidelines for Social Service

The three principal problems in giving educational aid — measuring progress, knowing what to do, knowing where to start — also apply to social service. Therefore, use the same approaches, but make several modifications.

When you measure progress, accept the fact that you cannot quantify it as readily as you can your educational aid. It will probably come more slowly, too. A feasible way to judge your progress in social service is on a case-by-case basis.

When you consider what to do, give special emphasis to those projects which most effectively help people to help themselves. Even more than your work in education, your work here should be as local as possible. Look for the small, modest situation. Steer clear of the grandiose projects.

When you determine where to start, avoid the government projects. Check the United Fund administrators in the area in which you have an interest. They usually have the best tie-ins with private groups.

Guidelines for Open Housing

Open housing is one of the most ticklish problems among urban difficulties. Federal, state, and local laws and court decisions on the subject still haven't overcome centuries-old prejudices. No businessmen's campaign will provide a widespread solution, either. But corporations have had success on a limited — sometimes even individual — basis.

Suggestions:

• Work locally wherever possible. Be alert for opportunities to act.

• Work through existing groups dedicated to open housing, but check their credentials carefully. An occasional group has turned out to be a front for a *block-busting* project.

- Lobby for local ordinances supporting open housing.
- Campaign for fair enforcement of open-housing laws.
- Work wherever possible through interested individual employees.
- Champion an individual employee's case when he's a victim of discrimination in housing — if he asks for help and after you have carefully investigated its merits.
- Avoid outside publicity on your role, but nevertheless let employees know about your corporate stand.
- Keep your corporate skirts clean. If top officials of your company live in restricted areas, watch out.
- Keep at it. Have patience.

Most companies prefer to steer clear of the question of open housing altogether. Can you — if you really face the urban crisis?

9 Black Power +
White Power =
Green Power

James Watts, president of the Impac Chemical Company, a Negro firm in Chicago, points out:

> There is a tremendous opportunity for blending. Black power and white power equals green power.

While the opportunity is there, the reality is not – yet. Impac Chemical is one of only 45,000 Negro businesses of a total of 5 million in the United States. If black people run less than 1 per cent of all businesses nationally, how do they do in predominantly Negro areas? Proportionately, not well there, either.

In Philadelphia less than 10 per cent of the companies are Negro owned. Even in an almost entirely black area like Harlem, Negroes own only 58 per cent of the stores. (But ironically, only about half those black store owners live in Harlem.) In the important commercial activity of food retailing, no more than 3 per cent of black people's food money is spent nationally in black grocery stores.

Robert B. McKersie, professor of industrial relations at the University of Chicago Graduate School of Business, says:

> Until more of these ghetto dwellers become employers rather than employees, they will remain outside the mainstream of our economic life and continue to despair of ever achieving full equality with whites.

To Richard M. Nixon, black capitalism is no radical concept, but the recognition that "with the ownership of the means of production goes power, prestige, security, the right to decide and to choose." It is a central point in his program for dealing with racial inequality.

In 1968, twenty-six senators, ranging in ideology from Senator Gaylord Nelson (Dem., Wis.) on the left to Senator John G. Tower (Rep., Tex.) on the right, sponsored an ambitious proposal for "community self-determination." The bill was drafted by the militant Congress of Racial Equality, on the advice of the Harvard Institute of Politics.

The measure strongly promotes Negro economic self-rule and has caused intense reactions pro and con. It may never get through Congress in its initial form (it advocates extensive special tax treatment for Negro-owned and managed firms), but the strong support for the bill indicates the magnetic qualities of black capitalism.

While some people – black and white alike – see in black capitalism an answer to the urban crisis because it may develop an economic power base for the ghetto, others criticize it. Many liberals don't think it can work. The voluminous report of the Kerner Commission on the 1967 riots devoted only three paragraphs to the subject, and essentially it recommends mere strengthening of existing programs.

Others fear that black capitalism will foster greater separatism. Indeed, CORE's national director, Ray Innis, has advocated it for that very reason. Psychologist Kenneth Clark foresees that such a development could lead to "gilded ghettos," which he views as little better than the present ghettos.

James L. Sundquist, Brookings Institution's senior fellow, contends that "well-intentioned" efforts to increase private industry in the ghettos are unlikely to amount to much more than the "tokenism" skeptically predicted by many Negroes.

In a Brookings report, Mr. Sundquist says flatly that ghetto self-sufficiency is impossible:

> If the prospects for ghetto industry in general are limited, the prospects for Negro-owned or Negro-operated industry – now so popular an idea – are even more so. Even if the ghetto market could be walled off,

in effect, through appeals to Negroes to "buy black," the market is not big enough to support significant manufacturing, and the number of white employees who could be replaced by black workers in retail and service establishments is limited.

For Negro companies in the ghetto to grow, they would have to compete successfully with companies outside the ghetto — and that, he expects, will take a long time.

But other experts on the subject agree with John H. Clay, president of Businessmen's Development Corporation, a Philadelphia organization supporting black capitalism:

> Our nation has tried primarily to rely upon social beneficence and assistance controlled by bodies outside the population affected, throwing away the vibrant lessons from our own history demonstrating time and time again that self-determination and individual initiative, in economic as well as political matters, breed capacity, responsibility, commitment, involvement, motivation . . . and results.

Black capitalism is mostly theory now because it remains a rather weak reed, but businessmen can help strengthen it; in fact they already are doing so.

Three Hurdles for Black Capitalism

The Negro finds himself more underrepresented in business management than in any other occupational category. Whereas more than 11 per cent of the white population work as managers, officials, and proprietors, the comparable figure for nonwhites is less than 3 per cent. Entrance into white-collar positions has been increasing faster for Negroes than it has for whites, but this isn't so in business management. If anything, blacks appear to be losing ground as a result of the attrition of Negro-owned firms that once served the now-disappearing segregated markets.

For example, the segregated market has been disappearing in insurance, where several sizable black companies have prospered. And black consumer-product companies' share of the Negro market is declining because of aggressive selling by large companies. Since most Negro-operated businesses still limit themselves to serving the needs of the segregated communities — carry-out stores, barber shops, and family grocery stores — they are small and likely to remain so. Few manufacturers and distributors have branched out from the ghetto markets.

Black capitalism faces many hurdles, but three that result from conditions of ghetto life stand out — the problems of small business generally and the lack of management skill and finance.

All small businesses — white and black — currently suffer challenge and change, especially in the city. Because of urban renewal, concentration of retailing in suburban shopping centers, and dispersal of industry to the urban perimeter, small-business opportunities in the city are diminishing regardless of who the would-be entrepreneurs are.

Cleveland typifies the problem. In the central city, population dropped from 915,000 to 876,000 between 1950 and 1965. In the same 15-year span, the metropolitan population jumped from 1.5 million to nearly 2 million. Downtown Cleveland's night life is virtually nonexistent. Only three department stores, six a decade ago, remain in business. Throughout the city, residential and highway construction lags. Air pollution can be seen as well as smelled. The Cuyahoga River, which splits the city, is so polluted that it is a fire hazard. It empties into Lake Erie, also polluted.

Mayor Carl Stokes has launched a Cleveland Now program whose $1.5 billion funding over the next decade will be used partly to try to foster black business. Mr. Stokes, reflecting the opinion of many large-city mayors says:

> Business and industry built these cities. If they are going to be rebuilt it will take the same investment and ingenuity that was originally employed.

Yet the most significant problem for Negroes is their general shortage of managerial skills and attitudes. As a race, black people have had scant exposure to business operations, technical experience, and managerial values necessary for economic success.

Limited entrepreneurial skill may mean failure even to a young Negro with drive and considerable technical know-how. Consider the case of a 40-year-old businessman who tried to make a go of his own auto-repair shop in a Texas city. He learned his basic technical skills with a new-car dealer in the area, becoming a top-flight mechanic by his thirtieth birthday. He next worked for a general shop for several years.

Finally, he started his own business in 1963. He struggled along for several years, doing a miscellaneous repair business. Although he didn't count himself a failure, he didn't get rich either. In fact, in moments of candid self-appraisal, he admitted that he made as much money working for others.

Then disaster struck. A fire destroyed his shop. Although he had insurance, it proved grossly inadequate to finance a fresh start. He went to the local Small Business Development Corporation and applied under Small Business Administration regulations for a loan, which was granted.

He rented larger quarters, installed better equipment than he had before, and took out adequate insurance. But things did not go well. Whereas he had formerly run virtually a one-man shop, with only occasional help from moonlighting mechanics during off-hours, he now had to have a full-time assistant because he needed more volume to meet his payments and to make economical use of his equipment. But he could not keep competent or reliable employees. And to get business, he took chances on marginal credit risks. Many were slow-pay, low-pay, or no-pay. In 1968, he had to declare bankruptcy.

Although financing was a problem for this man, his basic problem was lack of management skill — inadequate insurance in his first venture, a poor credit policy, unsatisfactory employees, and inexperience in managing a large enterprise in the second. He's back working for a new-car dealer now, managing the shop operation where he hopes to gain the experience to try again on his own.

Financing, however, limits many Negro businesses. For instance, an experienced and well-managed black construction company in Missouri wanted to handle a major renovation project in a ghetto. It had built garages, repaired and modernized homes, and had built a number of houses in its 20-year history, but it had never before tackled anything on this scale. The company didn't get the job because no Negro bank in the area had the resources to back it, and no other financing sources could be convinced that it could perform the job.

Incidentally, Negro-owned and managed banks are increasing in number, but they suffer from lower profitability than others — though deposits have grown faster — because of their greater costs in making small loans with high risks in the inner cities.

Then, how does black capitalism get moving? Three principal routes lead to success for most of the businesses that have formed: through sponsorship by a Negro group, through sponsorship by a white-managed organization, and through individual initiative in the classic example of free enterprise.

Sponsorship by a Negro Group

Typical programs supported principally by black development groups include these:

• Progress Aerospace Enterprises, Inc., is a Negro-initiated, owned, and managed company in Philadelphia. Founded by a Negro self-help program under the direction of the Rev. Mr. Leon Sullivan of the Zion Baptist Church in Philadelphia, the plant is one of a number of projects to come out of the church's "10-36" program in which members invest $10 a month for 36 months. (Another project: Opportunities Industrialization Centers, the job training organization.)

The plant manufactures components for the aerospace industry. It is expected to employ 160 by late 1969 and double that number in 1970. PAE received initial subcontracts from General Electric totaling $2.5 million, as well as a $522,000 contract from the U. S. Department of Labor to train workers for technical jobs. Most members of PAE management are Negroes. Profits from projects of the Zion Baptist Church flow back principally to the community in the form of charitable and educational benefits.

• Businessmen's Development Corporation, also founded in Philadelphia, takes a somewhat different approach. It is a profit-making development organization with more than 3,000 Negro stockholders (the majority of whom invest $10 a month) and an elected 35-man board of directors.

BDC's inner-city advisory services assist the businessman until he can present an application for a bank loan to fund his project. In some cases, BDC participates in the financing. In one 18-month period, loans processed through BDC totaled nearly $2 million. Average loan size was $16,000, although several were above $100,000 and one was for $400,000. The banks approved more than 60 per cent of the applications received through BDC.

The group's principles may be adapted for other cities. Hartford and Detroit already have similar organizations. Initial explorations were underway in mid-1968 in 30 other cities varying in size from 100,000 to 2 million.

• Harlem Commonwealth Council, working closely with CORE, provides some essential services that white businessmen have not yet offered. It started out in 1967 with a factoring operation, lending money at 6 per cent to Negro pharmacists caught in a credit squeeze because of late payments of state Medicaid bills. It plans to extend credit operations to Harlem doctors and dentists who face the same problem. It is also considering inventory loans to black businessmen. HCC draws on the expertise of McKinsey & Company, one of the nation's top management consulting firms, which charges no fee.

• In Rochester, New York, the militant FIGHT organization, involved at one time in a highly publicized battle with the city's largest employer, Eastman Kodak, has decided to go into business for itself − with the help of Xerox, the U. S. Labor Department, and the Rochester Business Opportunities Corporation (an organization of local businessmen supporting Negro entrepreneurship). The new company, Fighton, Inc., employs about 100 and produces low-voltage electrical transformers and metal standards. To give the company a chance to get on its feet, Xerox agreed to buy $500,000 of its output for each of the first two years. It has begun training Fighton's management and its work force with a $400,000 training grant from the Labor Department.

• The Negro Industrial and Economic Union is an organization that originated in Cleveland in 1965 and is now spreading to other cities. Its letterhead bears such names as Sammy Davis, Jr., the entertainer; Bill Russell, the basketball star; Jimmy Brown and John Wooten, former Cleveland Brown football stars.

The union has offices in New York, Los Angeles, Kansas City, and Cleveland and plans one in Washington. It has received a $520,000 grant from the Ford Foundation and another for $251,000 from the Commerce Department's Economic Development Administration.

It has helped such Negro firms as Magnificent Natural Products, Inc., a Los Angeles maker of shampoos and hair products aimed at the black market; Namax Builders, Inc., which rehabilitates slum homes in Cleveland ghettos; and New Breed Industries, Inc., a Brooklyn clothing manufacturer.

• Interracial Council for Business Opportunities is a New York City organization created by the Urban League and the Metropolitan Council of the American Jewish Congress. It finances promising projects through its capitalization, obtained largely from grants and gifts.

• "Accord in Detroit" concentrates on slum rehabilitation and other projects and raises money through sale of shares at $1 each.

• Poor People's Corporation was founded in 1965 in Jackson, Mississippi, by Jesse Morris, a Delaware-born Negro with a degree in economics from UCLA and a former field worker for the Student Nonviolent Coordinating Committee. It won initial financing from private sources.

The central facility in Jackson provides financial, technical, and marketing assistance for a group consisting of 12 producer cooperatives and one marketing cooperative, which sells what the producers make. Initial ventures have included a dress factory at Canton, Mississippi; a candle-making factory at West Point, Mississippi; a film-producing division named Southern Media; and Flute Publications, a book publishing operation specializing in books by home-state authors who have had difficulty getting published in the past.

The marketing cooperative provides the raw materials at cost to the producer cooperatives. In each producer cooperative are employees from the parent organization who provide the training and technical knowledge for the workers. The finished goods are returned to the marketing cooperative which sells to the public through direct mail and an expanding number of retail outlets.

• Business and Job Development Corporation is a nonprofit organization run by blacks but federally backed. It is Pittsburgh's first major effort to promote black capitalism. Since its founding in 1963, BJD's experience has mostly been with loan administration. It was initially organized to screen applicants and administer Small Business Administration loans. But its prime movers, James Jordon and Forrest Parr, began pushing for broader programs in 1965.

They secured the backing of Allegheny Conference, the powerful Pittsburgh business and civic establishment, and embarked on the development of an industrial park in a ghetto area. Westinghouse Electric Corporation was the first participant. It leased a $1.1 million plant to be built with BJD money and staffed with people from within the community. The facility will produce small industrial vehicles.

In this one park project BJD plans to create 970 jobs and 113 management positions.

Sponsorship by a White-Managed Organization

One of the goals of the Urban Coalition is to sponsor new businesses in ghettos. While much of this may be white-managed at the start, the idea is to encourage substantial minority-group management and ownership. The coalition is a national group — with branches in the major U. S. cities — of mayors, religious leaders, academicians, union officials, and businessmen seeking answers to the urban crisis.

To see how the coalition helps sponsor black capitalism, take the case of the Los Angeles branch. As co-chairman of that city's Urban Coalition and as head of its task force committee designed to bring industry into the ghettos, Harold Levitt takes substantial time from his job as vice president and senior partner at Dempsey-Tegeler & Company, a Los Angeles investment banking firm. He has made use of a hitherto obscure program of the U. S.

Labor Department, Special Impact, to bring into the inner city a wide variety of companies. For example:

• A & E Plastik Pak Corporation produces transparent meat trays. It built a $6.5 million plant, $1 million of it federally subsidized, to employ 335 hard-core jobless.

• Torite Enterprises, Inc., makes aircraft and automotive filters. Its plant cost $7.5 million, $1 million of which was supplied by the Labor Department. It also hired 335 hard-core unemployed.

• Bubble-Up Corporation, a soft drink producer, built a $6.5 million facility, $1 million of it through a Labor Department grant. Employment is projected at 275.

• Udico Corporation, a producer of electrical appliances and toweling, erected an $8 million plant, more than $1 million of which came from the government. It employs 360 disadvantaged people.

• Sahagen Industries, Inc., an electronics manufacturer, invested $8 million in a new plant, $1 million of it granted to the company by the Labor Department. Sahagen hired 250 hard-core jobless.

• Four firms, with a federal outlay of more than $3.3 million combined with their own capital commitments of $27.5 million, will renovate an empty jail in a Mexican-American area, to turn it into a factory employing 1,800. Sacoma Companies, Inc., will produce furniture and home furnishings. Monarch Electronics International, Inc., will operate an electronic assembly facility. Barrier, Inc., will provide plastic auto-camper and container manufacturing occupations. Lady Fair Kitchens, Inc., will produce kitchen cabinets and wooden pallets.

Although Impact has as its major thrust the creation of jobs, its implementation through the Urban Coalition has proved effective in establishing ghetto industries. While a few hard-line black militants in Los Angeles consider it merely another form of white plantationism, H. C. "Chad" McClellan, president of the Los Angeles Management Council of Merit Employment, stresses that the stock option and profit-sharing aspects of the program mean that "everybody will have a chance to own a part [of a company]."

Other typical projects backed primarily by "white establishments" include these:

• With an investment of $1.7 million, Aerojet-General Corporation has set up Watts Manufacturing Company in the Watts section of Los Angeles. The plant is under Negro management, and its first order was a $2.5 million contract to make military tents. In 1968 it provided 500 jobs.

• Control Data Corporation has established an electronics manufacturing operation in a low-income area of Minneapolis. It is housed in a new plant. About 235 inner-city people employed there produce peripheral controllers (electronic devices used in the company's computer systems).

Control Data will also locate a facility in a low-income area of the District of Columbia. A temporary facility will employ about 150 to 200 persons, with preference for underemployed residents. They will move to a new plant, expected to be completed by the summer of 1970, where employment eventually will reach 300. In addition to manufacturing activity, the new building will house a Control Data Institute. The initial phase of the manufacturing operation at the temporary facility will produce electronic modules and electronic subassemblies.

• Lockheed Aircraft Corporation has established a subsidiary plant to make aircraft ground-support equipment in San Antonio's Mexican-American district. General Dynamics Corporation already has a new metal and woodworking operation there — products range from shipping pallets to aircraft structures.

• Avco Corporation is building a plant to handle the company's printing needs in Boston's Roxbury Negro area. E G & G, Inc., the company that triggers atomic-bomb blasts for the Atomic Energy Commission, is putting a metal fabrication plant in the same neighborhood.

• IBM will make computer cables in a plant in Brooklyn's Bedford-Stuyvesant Negro ghetto.

• Brown Shoe Company plans to build a plant in St. Louis' Jeff-Vander-Lou slum area.

• Hough Manufacturing Company, Inc., a Negro-managed — and eventually wholly Negro-owned — metalworking plant in Cleveland is backed to the tune of $300,000 by Warner & Swasey, the big Cleveland machine tool and equipment firm. Hough is being built from the nucleus of a struggling Negro company.

• Shearson, Hammill Company, a Wall Street brokerage concern, has opened a branch in Harlem, the first branch there of a major member of the New York Stock Exchange or the American Stock Exchange. The manager is a Negro, Russell L. Goings, Jr.

• Congaree Iron & Steel Company, founded in 1958 by W. F. Threatt, in Congaree, South Carolina, is now predominantly Negro-managed. With the help of the Ford Foundation, Mr. Threatt has agreed to set up an employee trust fund to enable Negro employees to acquire a sizable stake in ownership and profits.

The Self-Starters

Although space doesn't permit the listing of even a representative sampling of the 45,000 Negro businesses, note that there are black cleaning firms, garage and repair shops, gas stations and trucking companies (the all-Negro New Jersey Truckers Association lists 200 members). But also waiting to serve are black law firms, accountants, building contractors, stationers, caterers, hardware stores, fuel-oil dealers, travel agencies, security-guard services, printers (Chaucer Press, Inc., in New York is owned by a graduate of the Harvard Business School), banks, insurance brokers, and insurance companies.

A growing number of black manufacturers make fine products. These firms include sporting-goods makers such as the Green Power Foundation in California that is building a national reputation with a baseball bat dubbed the Watts Walloper; food firms like Baltimore's H. G. Parks Company, Inc., famed for its

"More Parks Sausages, Mom" commercials; and pharmaceutical and cosmetic companies such as Riverton Laboratories, Inc., of Newark, New Jersey, that was founded in a kitchen 20 years ago and now grosses more than $2 million a year.

Dot Laboratories, Inc., in Harlem is an example of the increasingly numerous self-starting outfits prospering on sub-contracting — both for the government and private companies. Says Errol Jones, president:

> Giving black-owned firms in the Negro community an opportunity to bid on contracts can create payrolls, help stabilize the neighborhood, and give other black people an economic success story to emulate.

The foregoing are examples of the participation and aid which the white business establishment can give. The next chapter follows up with the specifics of this blending — so that black power and white power truly can equal green power.

 # Capitalism, White and Black

Fifty-two large organizations participated in a unique Suppliers Opportunity Day in September, 1968, at the Hawthorne Works of Western Electric Company in Chicago.

Western Electric, the Chicago Urban League, and the Chicago Economic Development Corporation sponsored a trade fair where 125 minority-group businesses learned how they could become suppliers to big business. Some of the small black companies were well established; others were trying to get the order that would launch them as going enterprises.

In a morning session, speakers representing a wide range of large business and industrial activities explained their needs that could be met by small businesses. All of the 52 large firms had key purchasing men at the clinic, and the afternoon was devoted to business discussion (and some on-the-spot transactions) at individual company booths.

Garland Guice, director of the Economic Development unit that served as co-sponsor, said:

> The mood is changing in Negro communities. Negro business wants a piece of the action ... which means an equitable share in the capitalistic system.

This approach, which has been adapted in other cities, is just one of many techniques that business and industry can use to foster black capitalism. But before you determine what you can do in this area, take into account these factors:

1. Most Negro-owned businesses are in the service and trade fields and are very small. They compare in size with many other enterprises as they were 30 to 40 years ago and are conducted at a rather low level of efficiency, organization, and profitability. Most minority-group members have not been part of the American industrial and economic revolution which has propelled American business efficiency. As a result, the Negro businessman is struggling to survive, despite the generally prosperous and booming state of the U.S. economy.

2. Many forces are currently stimulating black capitalism — civil-rights groups, religious organizations, foundations, and the simple desire to participate in the benefits of free enterprise. The motivation of some of these groups may not prove healthy because, with few exceptions, business has not flourished for ideological reasons. It prospers when it fills a practical need. When civil-rights, religious, and other sponsors can mesh their ideological motivations with practical needs, they may succeed. When they cannot, they may fail.

3. More often than not, many Negro businessmen symbolize frustration and hopelessness rather than achievement, success, and leadership — in marked contrast to their white counterparts. As a result, Negro parents as a rule tend to discourage their children from pursuing business careers, especially as entrepreneurs.

With these assumptions as background, the following ten basic principles become more understandable, as developed by Businessmen's Development Corporation, the Philadelphia organization formed to spur black capitalism:

1. Total control (not mere participation) must be lodged within the hands of achievers among the special population or area served. "Mixed" boards take away what should be

the full responsibility of the black businessman. The people involved must have the power to hire and fire their own officers.

2. The development instrument itself must be a profit instrument, free to plow back profits for its own development, free to attract and reward superior capacity.

3. The organization's strength is based upon consensus or agreement among those who share the commitment, avoiding the need to seek "popular" approval, which waters down commitment. The ghetto now has far too pervasive a structure of "laid on" groups and organizations struggling for backing (and whose resources go for staffs) because they have not grown within, drawing commitment from the people.

4. From the outset, the goal must not be limited to helping present businessmen to survive in the ghetto. Instead, the goal should be to prepare and equip the more dynamic and capable individuals to operate as successfully and broadly as their skills can extend. The inner-city ethnic market is a poor market.

5. The development group must aim at quality, not quantity.

6. Instead of lower standards for the Negro (for loans, etc.), there must be dynamic, sustained efforts to prepare men to meet the standards that the business community has found necessary. Far worse than not getting a loan is to get it and fail because of poor preparation.

7. There must be no ceilings on loan size, income potentials, goals.

8. The inner city must be ready to seize advantages, not wait supinely for opportunity. For example, the development of Negro-owned auto dealerships should not have to wait for Detroit initiative.

9. The approach must elevate and recognize the inner city's own expertise. The know-how from outside must be on tap, not on top.

10. Far from being separatist, the program must have strong links to major outside power sources who extend funds or license production and distribution know-how on the basis of what's in it for them.

What Business Can Do

If the white establishment wants to make meaningful contributions to black capitalism, the aid should be offered with the understanding that the Negroes want control, profitability, growth from within, attainable goals which are nevertheless not too low, quality not quantity, the same standards as for white-controlled business, the opportunity to develop their own expertise, and the opportunity to have ties and contacts outside the ghetto area.

Within this framework, we will examine how white capitalism can spur black capitalism in three broad areas — applying know-how, infusing capital, and opening new opportunities.

Applying Know-How

A Howard University project illustrates one method of teaching know-how. Funded by the Commerce Department, Howard analyzed small, black-owned dry cleaners in the Washington area. After determining the greatest problems, it initiated standardized procedures for:

1. Physical appearance
2. Quality control
3. Accounting systems
4. Employee and employer benefit programs
5. Employee training
6. Customer service expansion
7. Cooperative buying of wholesale supplies

Capital Drycleaners Association was formed as the vehicle to organize the shop owners, initially with some 65 dues-paying members. CDA soon made progress in six areas: improvement of the physical appearance of the shops; review of records; insurance; employer and employee training; advertising; and publishing a newsletter. Planned is further standardization of operational procedures and marketing techniques.

Abraham S. Venable, director of the Affirmative Action Programs Staff of the Commerce Department's Business and Defense Services Administration, says:

> We have been greatly pleased with the initial success of the dry cleaning project . . . . Response from the individual dry cleaners has been enthusiastic. Cooperation of established trade associations, which represented a big question mark, has been most gratifying.

The Howard University-Commerce Department project seeks to apply know-how across a broad spectrum. Most individual companies, however, would do better to confine their assistance to a more modest range of advice. The following are modest, but effective, programs.

• Jewel Companies, Inc., a large Chicago-based retail food chain, has set out to help close the managerial gap in its field. Recognizing that the key to success in food distribution lies in winning customer acceptance, Jewel executives are assisting black businessmen in such critical areas as packaging, quality control, and promotion.

• Some white companies have helped Negroes get into business by identifying activities that only specialists know could exist. For instance, American Oil Company has helped establish a Negro entrepreneur in the retrieving of used tires from service stations. His reward: weekly fees from the stations he serves.

• In 1963 a group of successful white and black executives got together to discuss new ways to help Negroes improve themselves economically. Out of that meeting came the Interracial Council for Business Opportunity which offers free management-consulting services to Negroes who want to go into business for themselves or to improve the business they are already in. The consulting services are provided by lumberyard owners, restauranteurs, CPA's, shopkeepers, and hundreds of other volunteers in New York, Newark, Washington, Los Angeles, and New Orleans.

- Sponsors of Junior Achievement have backed the first such enterprises in Harlem where 40 black youngsters have started up companies named J. A. Tex and Soul Crafts.

At first, the black capitalist usually needs assistance in bookkeeping and establishing the fundamental financial controls. Once his enterprise appears a going concern, he needs advice on more special subjects, such as gauging his markets, training employees, and setting up quality-control programs.

The counselor's role may shift at this time from that of a professional giving technical help to one of a confidant providing support on a host of matters. While this role proves valuable and usually effective, guard against the Negro's becoming too dependent on the advisor. For this reason, management-assistance programs should be aimed toward creating the capacity within the client to identify and solve his own problems.

Developing the relationship that fosters a balanced counseling usually proves difficult. The typical white businessman has never been in a ghetto, has not worked in small business, and may not have the time to give the intensive help required. On the other hand, the client may hold misconceptions about the role of the consultant. He may think that the advisor is available to mind the store while he goes to the bank or to repair a machine.

Suspicion on both sides isn't uncommon. Sometimes the advisor, delegated to perform the counseling job by his own company, makes it only too clear that he does it, at best, for recognition from his employer or, at worst, because he has to. The client may show his disbelief that a really sincere counselor truly wants to help. Proof that the advice improves the efficiency of the business or brings in more customers is the best way to put the relationship on a footing of mutual trust.

The presence of some sort of organization in the black community that brings counselor and client together can smooth the road dramatically. Harlem Commonwealth Council, the National Urban League and many others mentioned in Chapter 9 perform this function.

The question of whether the client should pay for the consulting services often comes up. While it would make sense to put such a relationship on a business basis, most black clients can't afford to pay anything significant. One solution may be to ask the recipient to contribute to community development in lieu of payment. In a program developed in St. Paul, black capitalists — retailers mostly — trained unemployed youth in their stores.

Business schools occupy a particularly advantageous position to provide advice. Columbia, Stanford, Chicago, Harvard, and other business schools have established training programs and workshops for black businessmen, with instruction and counseling provided by faculty members and students. Corporations can use their influence to spur laggard business schools into action.

Know-how can be applied in forms other than intermittent counseling. During the shakedown, the white business can set up a black subsidiary or sponsor a new business in its industry; then spin it off when it's ready to fly on its own. Or a corporation's marketing staff could conduct a market analysis for a community organization, or the white-managed company could handle the legal and other work involved in establishing a trade association or a nonprofit development corporation.

Infusing Capital

If management know-how is black capitalism's most pervasive problem, money is its most exasperating. Negro businessmen often have more trouble getting financing than do white entrepreneurs because black businessmen experience a higher failure rate than do their white counterparts, for the reasons already mentioned.

Yet financing sources do exist, and you can render a major service to black capitalism by helping the Negro businessman to explore all the possibilities.

The first and most obvious source is the bank. Not all banks will cooperate because they see the risk associated with lending to a small business.

However, some banks have a policy of supporting black capitalism. First Pennsylvania Banking & Trust Company is an example. In its loan program, it minimizes the risk by thorough investigation and screening and — once a loan is granted — surveillance. Although it admittedly accepts loan applications in the Negro community that would be rejected if they came from other Philadelphia areas, the bank reports that the default rate has been less than 1 per cent.

The extra effort costs the banks money. At least one big-city institution has proposed to several of its large corporate depositors that they accept one percentage point less in interest to underwrite the administrative and reserve requirements of its loan program for Negro business.

Negro banks have grown and constitute a potential funding source for black capitalism. In some cases, the white establishment has given substantial support to Negro banks through deposits and even guarantees of loans. Southern California Edison Company pledges funds to Los Angeles' black-operated Bank of Finance which aggressively promotes Negro economic development. A similar institution, Freedom National Bank in Harlem, gets broad support from white corporations and New York City.

A financing source combining Negro and white banks, plus a black-capitalism development organization, is provided by an arm of the Interracial Council for Business Opportunity in New York City. It created ICBO Fund, Inc., whose objective is to provide additional funds for disadvantaged areas.

Working with Freedom National and three other major downtown banks — Chase Manhattan, Bankers Trust, and Chemical Bank New York Trust Company — ICBO agrees to absorb 50 per cent of any loss on loans made to Negro businessmen whose credit application it approves. The borrowing company becomes a client of the council, receiving free consulting services from its staff during the life of the loan.

With capital raised from foundations and corporations, ICBO Fund expects to guarantee more than $1 million in loans under this program alone, in addition to its normal aid in arranging loans without guaranty.

Insurance companies — black and white — possess enormous financing capabilities, but the nature of their business necessitates a conservative approach on loans. The insurance companies that pledged the billion-dollar program for investment in cities have had difficulty in locating suitable candidates. They even compete among themselves for the few loan "plums."

Another loan source is the federal government. Small Business Administration's Equal Opportunity Loans flowed at the rate of about $3 million each month in fiscal 1968 to spur black capitalism. But, by comparison, the SBA distributes approximately $300 million each year under its other loan programs. One of SBA's problems with Equal Opportunity Loans has been in persuading commercial banks to participate. In regular loan activities, SBA has been able to achieve bank participation in about 20 per cent of its cases.

Foundations provide another loan source. In a major change from its past investment policies, the Ford Foundation has begun investing directly in ghetto industries and other enterprises likely to yield significant social benefits rather than only capital gains. The foundation's trustees have earmarked $10 million for such investments. Its total portfolio exceeds $3 billion, in Ford Motor and other blue chips. It expects to recover most of its socially motivated investments for reinvestment.

Some local arms of the National Urban Coalition, the New York group among them, have formed economic development corporations to help finance new ventures. A few local Negro churches have done likewise. White businessmen have formed seed-money organizations to perform this function in several locations. A promising example is the Rochester Business Opportunities Corporation. Some 60 corporations had pledged about $250,000 by late 1968 to help spur loans through Rochester banks and the SBA.

A white-managed corporation may provide the financing, particularly for Negro dealerships or franchises. Chrysler Corporation, for instance, helps to finance some of its Negro dealers with working-capital loans or leased facilities. Until 1967, only one dealership among the U.S. auto industry's network of 30,000 was Negro-owned. About a year later, ten were doing business.

For financing reasons, some white firms may wish to set up black subsidiaries or affiliates. The parent company can eventually sell all or part of its interest to Negro businessmen. For example, E G & G plans to reduce its holding in its Boston ghetto plant to 50 per cent in five years and to 25 per cent in 20 years through distribution of stock for management options, an employee stock purchase plan, and a public offering aimed at Boston's black community. Fairchild Hiller Corporation intends to hold only 10 per cent of Fairmicco, a Washington firm it set up to train and hire men for sheet metal work and other jobs. A community group that helped fund the concern will hold another 10 per cent, with the remainder sold in a public offering aimed at Negroes.

The use of equity capital shows some promise of helping black businessmen solve their money difficulties, without the burden of meeting interest or repayment schedules. Aiding in this has been the formation of Small Business Investment Corporations in several cities under the aegis of SBA. Two of these, Accord in Detroit, and Businessmen's Development Corporation in Philadelphia, sold stock at low prices for reinvestment in fledgling enterprises. A few Negro companies have tried stock sales on their own, with mixed results.

Opening New Opportunities

Although providing financing is a major way to open new opportunities for black capitalism, additional methods exist:

• The Chicago Economic Development Corporation acts as a broker through which area corporations establish suppliers. The Suppliers Opportunity Day, mentioned at the beginning of this chapter, was one of its projects. Inner City Development Corporation, a CEDC arm, plans several small industrial parks where Negro-owned manufacturing companies will locate.

• In San Francisco, Plan of Action for Challenging Times (PACT), founded by Negro leaders, operates a business development center, among other things.

• The U. S. Department of Commerce has held clinics for Negroes on franchising and acts as a clearing house for interested companies and individuals.

• Joint black and white projects often prove feasible. For instance, Harlem investors and the Hotel Corporation of America plan to build a first-class motor hotel of 230 to 300 rooms in the New York ghetto, the largest private commercial venture ever undertaken in Harlem.

• White trade associations are helping their black counterparts by more closely involving them with the usually larger, more knowledgeable, and richer white group.

• Retailing ideas abound. One is a Sew-A-Mat, consisting of a mill ends and remants shop and a sewing machine rental service. Women can come in, buy quality fabrics at bargain prices, receive instructions on how to make clothes and slipcovers, then sew them on machines renting for about 25 cents an hour. Another retailing venture catching on in disadvantaged areas: do-it-yourself furniture stores selling unfinished items which buyers must carry home, assemble, and paint. These shops require only modest capital.

To see how you may help open up new opportunities, let's examine the Rochester Business Opportunities Corporation, both because it has enjoyed considerable success and because great care and thought went into its formation. RBOC sprang from a suggestion by Eastman Kodak officials in late 1967. Other major Rochester employers, such as Xerox and Sybron Corporation, as well as minority-group organizations, joined in; and RBOC began operating in 1968. Its staff includes a general manager and an accountant whose job is to help RBOC's Business Development Committee to screen loan applicants and to assist them in developing proposals.

RBOC's 28-member board includes many of the blue-chip names in the Rochester business community, plus several Negroes – a restaurant proprietress, the owner of a beauty and barber shop supply house, and two insurance agents – and a grocery store owner of Puerto Rican origin.

RBOC's more than 60 corporate supporters had given or pledged some $250,000 by late 1968. The money is used as seed capital for financing new businesses. These include general contractors, a grocery store, auto-body repair shops, a sign painter, building-maintenance firms, a plastic-molding company, a beauty-shop operator, and trucking-equipment companies, to name only a few of the organizations.

RBOC requires that most of the would-be entrepreneurs contribute a certain amount of equity to their businesses. Many of the newly formed enterprises incorporate profit-sharing plans for employees; some expect eventually to distribute stock to their people.

In considering proposals for a new venture, the principal criteria of the organization's Business Development Committee are the soundness of the market for its product or service, its potential for making a profit, and the opportunity for growth. The cost of the financing and the creation of jobs are of secondary interest. To cut red tape, any venture needing less than $2,000 may proceed with organizing after receiving committee endorsement, but before RBOC's board has passed on it.

Another RBOC committee, Technical Advisory, calls on experts to help new business get going. Experts come from the supporting corporations, the local Harvard Business School Association, and the Rochester group of certified public accountants. The CPA's have drawn up a financial model, including a *pro forma* balance sheet, a profit-and-loss statement, and a cash-flow statement. They also assist fledgling businessmen in making proposals and help them in setting up their books once they are in business.

RBOC sees the following factors as ingredients for success:

• It fosters minority-group enterprise not only in the traditional segregated businesses but also in manufacturing and service fields where the black capitalists have a chance to overcome their historical market barriers.

• It has broadly based support from the white business community.

• It has good financial resources – to supply seed money for bank and government loans.

• It bears no taint of white paternalism because respected minority-group organizations participate.

• It has an adequate and permanent administrative structure, providing a meeting ground for the groups and individuals involved and an auditing mechanism for the new businesses.

• It makes sure that the venture has a sustaining market that can produce a profit before it backs a proposition.

• It provides managerial aid and consulting assistance.

• It requires the black capitalists to contribute their own equity money when they can and encourages them to offer profit-sharing and stock option plans to their employees, thus promoting self-respect and economic independence.

Where Do We Go from Here?

You can locate black-owned companies through the local office of the Urban League, the Small Business Administration, probably your own city hall, Negro churches, or the advertising manager of the local Negro newspaper.

Yet many white businessmen have been politely turned down in their efforts to foster black capitalism — and sometimes not politely. The white capitalist often feels damned if he does and damned if he doesn't. If he ignores the struggling black business-man, he may be called *callous* or even *racist*. If he leaps into the ghetto with offers of help, he may hear rude advice to stick to his plush office and try to solve white problems.

Although the white man may be a professional in business matters, he's usually an amateur in racial affairs. When he decides to make his expertise available in the ghettos, he's wise to adopt a new role — probably a subordinate one. For instance, a business-men's group in a southwestern city have pledged a substantial sum to stimulate black capitalism, but strictly with no strings attached. Furthermore, they will offer managerial and other aid only if asked.

At first, a white manager may become uncomfortable, even angered, if in his sincere desire to help he is asked to defer to the wishes of inexperienced black businessmen or to the policies of militant civil-rights organizations. Yet, some whites have overcome their misgivings and have developed a partnership of equals.

Chicago University's Professor Robert B. McKersie points out:

> In city after city what is most needed for Negro economic development is a catalyst to put the pieces together — the capital is available, the markets are waiting to be tapped, and the individuals with entrepreneurial potential are on hand. Obviously, U. S. corporate enterprise possesses the managerial capability to be that catalyst.

Despite the problems, there's reason for optimism. The growth rate of businesses owned by minorities doubled between June and September in 1968. Minority-owned enterprises were formed at the rate of 2,000 a year in June; 4,000 a year in September. Specialists in new business formations say the rate could reach 20,000 a year by the 1970's.

A Better Place
In which
To Live

Of the many solutions needed for the urban crisis, three possess top priorities – more and improved jobs for the disadvantaged, higher quality education for them, and a better place for them to live.

Of those three solutions, the last may prove the most difficult to accomplish. That's because such a solution encompasses a total environment – better housing, better cities for the housing, and cleaner air, purer water, and greater quiet for the cities. But this poses problems because of our lagging technologies for dealing with environmental questions.

If an eighteenth-century carpenter or mason could rise from his grave, he would have little trouble picking up his craft today. This situation has no parallel in other industries or in agriculture in the U. S. Although some cities have been planned since the urban way of life began, most have grown up with woefully inadequate forethought, and the science of city planning remains in its adolescence. The technologies involved in the control of noise and water and air pollution have only reached childhood, at best, because noise and pollution have presented overwhelming difficulties only since this century began.

Furthermore, most people, not just the disadvantaged, seek a better environment, so the demand for improvement is staggering. Take just one example: Some experts believe that the nation's

housing needs, 1968 through 1975, total 18 million new units —
which is about 6 million more than the construction industry,
operating at its present peak levels, can supply.

In addition, a wholesale attack on environmental problems
involves construction as a common denominator. The cost of
construction had gone up 18 per cent in the last few years,
whereas the bulk of manufactured products have risen only about
3 per cent.

The Dilemma in Housing

Raising the quality and quantity of low-income housing while
still lowering the cost is the main problem in providing for the
disadvantaged. Most experts in housing despair of the government's ever finding the answer. Despite billions poured into
federal housing and urban renewal programs over 30 years, 8
million American families still can't afford a decent home,
according to a White House report.

In one ten-year period of the Urban Renewal Program, the
government demolished about 120,000 dwelling units with a
median rental value of $40 a month. During the same period, the
government built 25,000 to 30,000 new units with a median rental
value of $180 a month. The poor were evicted from their crowded
and unsatisfactory housing into housing even less satisfactory and
more crowded. The people who could afford to pay $180 a month
enjoyed subsidized housing at public expense.

Nor is it clear that the private construction industry can do
dramatically better. As presently constituted, the industry is
largely composed of small enterprises, usually under-financed and
over-burdened with obsolete building codes and union rules.

Brightness does appear on the horizon, however. A whole new
approach to housing construction got underway in September,
1968, when President Johnson named Edgar F. Kaiser, the West
Coast industrialist, to organize a Comsat-like corporation which
will provide a vehicle for private industry to invest its resources of
talent and money in a massive attack on the nation's slums.
Authorized as part of the sweeping Housing and Urban Development Act passed in July, 1968, the new National Corporation for

Housing Partnerships aims to finance and build as many as 50,000 new units a year – more than the government program completed in 1968 and ten times the output of Levitt & Sons, the nation's largest private builder.

The 16-man Board of Incorporators, which includes Mr. Kaiser as chairman, plus businessmen, bankers, labor leaders, and educators, hopes to round up $50 million in pledges from major corporations. Unlike Comsat, the housing company plans no public sale of stock. The $50 million, the supporters' prestige, and federal credit guarantees will give the organization borrowing power of about $2 billion.

Housing construction will be carried out in partnership with local builders, and the new corporation's investment in any project must not exceed 25 per cent of the total expense unless local funds cannot be raised.

In the past, both builders and construction unions have been reluctant to gear up for low-cost housing because of the on-again, off-again quality of government programs. The 1968 law, by contrast, not only contains authorizations for three years but sets a ten-year goal to build at least 6 million housing units. The public-private housing partnership will provide a bridge between government and industry, much like Comsat in the communications field or the National Alliance of Businessmen in the field of jobs for the disadvantaged.

Revolutionizing Building Techniques

And a few technological developments hold promise of revolutionizing the building of housing units. Ironically, three of the most dramatic are burgeoning under the aegis of the Department of Defense. Every year, the Department of Defense builds between 8,000 and 10,000 housing units for officers, enlisted men, and their families. In an advanturous program of securing new technology and lower costs for its construction ventures, it awarded contracts for three housing proposals.

The department plans to take the best technological innovations from each of the three winning proposals, combine them with other techniques and mesh them into one industrialized building system. Two hundred units — probably two-story row houses — will be built initially at George Air Force Base northeast of Los Angeles. If the program is successful there, the same building system will be used by many contractors on other military-housing sites.

The Department of Defense specified that solutions should be applicable to the high-density housing requirements of urban centers. Recognizing the technological lag in much of the construction industry, the department also sought bids from electronic and aerospace corporations. The contract winners were:

• The Techcrete system of Architect Carl Koch who teamed with Kaiser Industries, Westinghouse, and Battelle Memorial Institute. The Koch firm has had 20 years' experience in designing and constructing several kinds of prefabricated structures, and Techcrete, the concrete assembly system, has already been used in several buildings.

• The University of Michigan and Aerojet-General's filament-wound container system. The university's Architectural Research Laboratory and the company's Structural Products Division put forward the most technologically advanced proposal of the three winners. They propose to use filament-winding, a method developed by the aerospace industry for making rocket-engine cases. The filaments would be 80 per cent glass and 20 per cent polyester resin. Houses will be produced like cocoons by spinning the filaments around a steel mandrel. Although many shapes can be spun with the system, the research team conservatively chose a rectangle, open at both ends, that can be stacked two-high.

• General Electric's conventional approach. GE's dramatic cost savings result from improvements in conventional home-building technology and site-engineering practices. It proposes a structural system, an integrated set of building components to fit that system, an on-site mobile factory unit, complete fabrication procedures with labor costs and jobs fully detailed, interior plans and site plans for small housing communities, as well as an extensive analysis of "human factors" in design.

Although the three winners' solutions differ greatly, the similarities will have the greatest impact on the construction industry. All three advocate on-site fabrication of structural components; the use of prefabricated subsystems; use of a total "environment system" or system-building approach to the construction and design process; innovations in solid waste and sewage disposal; changes in labor practices; and extensive innovations in site preparations and utilities engineering. In addition, they each have achieved major cost savings in materials and erection, as well as reduced expense of labor from the current 40 to 50 per cent of the cost of building to about 25 per cent.

There are other building innovations. Against a background of construction-industry skepticism, union suspicion, ghetto cynicism, and bureaucratic obstructionism, U. S. cities have begun to experiment with "instant housing" — the factory-built module, version of the mobile home.

Projects have sprung up in many cities: Chicago; Rochester; Detroit; San Antonio; Amherst, Massachusetts; Vicksburg, Mississippi; Richmond, California; Henrietta, New York; Cleveland; Cincinnati; Akron; Buffalo; Syracuse; Lansing; Washington, D. C.; St. Louis; New Haven; Hartford; and Newark.

For $350 down and $125 a month, Chicago ghetto dwellers can buy four-bedroom units for $14,500. Such firms as Guerdon Industries, Inc., National Homes Corporation, Stirling Homex Corporation, and others are pioneering in this development.

Approval is not unanimous, however. Some Negro militants call them "cracker boxes." Members of Cornell University's Center for Housing and Environmental Studies warn, "The result could well be the mass production of mediocrity."

Yet, proponents do point to savings: in construction financing because of time saved; in mass-production economies; in ability to manufacture homes with year-round immunity to weather; and in more efficient use of skilled labor which is in critically short supply.

Rise of the New Cities

Sufficient low-income housing, high in standards and reasonable in cost, will prove useless, however, if the cities in which they are built don't improve in quality.

Experts now say that in the remaining years of this century we'll have to build the equivalent of all that has been built in America since the pilgrims set foot on Plymouth Rock. If this growth goes ahead in the largely untrammeled way of the past, the urban crisis of today may seem like bucolic serenity compared with what the situation could be by the year 2000.

Fortunately, planning for new cities is on the rise. All across America, private businesses compete to rebuild existing cities and to construct new towns. Every month we add 300,000 people (a city about the size of El Paso) to our population. We make a Philadelphia-sized addition every year.

John B. Turner, Jr., president of Friendswood Development Company, a subsidiary of Humble Oil, states:

> [New towns] may well be the way for metropolitan areas to absorb the tremendous growth we expect without repeating past mistakes.

Alcoa, interested in building new cities within existing cities, had 11 major projects underway in mid-1968. Alcoa president John D. Harper says:

> A corporation can't exist in a vacuum; it has to accept the responsibility of citizenship.

And rehabilitating dilapidated urban areas is a way he believes that Alcoa can meet this responsibility.

The term *new town* refers to a total community, with acreage for residential, commercial, industrial, and educational uses. The employment base, more than anything else, differentiates it from other real-estate subdivisions.

The new towns proliferating today in the U. S. aim to make the highest use of available land. Whether they choose to cluster homes closely together or pile them on top of each other, they provide common *green space*. By subdividing a new town into villages with a central core, planners are bringing back to life the congeniality of small-town living. On the other hand, by attracting industry, offices and big stores to the central town, they take on the excitement of a city.

Theoretically, most new towns, when complete, will provide nearly enough jobs to support their populations. But in practice, many people living in a new town continue to work elsewhere, and many people who work there won't move there to live.

Yet for those who do live and work in the new town, tedious commuting is gone. There's little need to "get away to the country" because you're already there. Odds are you will have only a short walk or drive to church, supermarket, office, golf course, riding stable, theater, or fishing lake.

A few of the new towns are already being built.

Clear Lake City — Bayport, Texas

This residential, commercial, educational, and industrial complex near Houston had to face — and solve — many problems.

In 1938, Humble bought for mineral value a tract of land called the West Ranch from a flamboyant Texas multimillionaire, Jim West. The property totaled about 30,000 acres. By the mid-1950's a successful oil exploration program had defined the productive acreage, leaving 23,000 acres for other use.

Humble went to Lehman Brothers in New York for advice. Lehman recommended the development of an industrial complex that would create new, long-term markets for Humble products produced in its nearby Baytown refinery. Lehman further suggested that once the industrial activity had created a sufficient job base that Humble develop a new town. Humble agreed, but events transposed the order of development.

In 1961 the National Aeronautics and Space Administration decided to build its Manned Spacecraft Center on a site selected in Humble's West Ranch properties. This caused Humble to build Clear Lake City, the residential and commercial part of the new development. Construction of Clear Lake began in 1962, as did construction of the Space Center. Two years later, Bayport — the heavy industrial side of the new town — got started, to assure a broad economic base for the area and to avoid total dependency on NASA for future growth.

At first, residential activity bogged. Only medium-priced, single-family units were built — no apartments, no town houses.

Although well constructed, the homes were too similar. That has been remedied, and apartments and town houses are being built and rented as fast as they're completed. Residential lot sales exceeded 600 in 1968 and were expected to top 1,000 annually by 1970.

Although the success of Clear Lake City needed several years and some turning around to accomplish, the 8,750-acre Bayport industrial complex started fast, kept its momentum and in 1968 was five years ahead of schedule. Humble's subsidiary started by building a channel to give industries access to 29,000 miles of navigable rivers and inland waterways. Large chemical, cement, aircraft, and electronics firms have selected Bayport sites.

Columbia, Maryland

Halfway between Washington and Baltimore is rising the new town of Columbia, which in 1968 already had a population of more than 3,000 after only one and one-half years of existence. Eventually it will have 110,000 residents.

From the first, James Rouse, a mortgage banker and developer of shopping centers, left little to chance. Years before the first spade of dirt was turned in 1966, teams of specialists examined the ways in which people live with people in an urban environment. They set up an economic model that guides the town's development.

After careful consideration, The Rouse Company picked a site midway between Baltimore, basically a manufacturing city with an excellent port, and Washington, basically a research and development city, aside from government. A new interstate highway, planned for completion about 1970, will improve the accessibility even more.

By the beginning of 1969, 17 industries had selected locations in Columbia. Eastern Products Corporation, a manufacturer of drapery hardware, was already operating a plant there and expects to employ 2,000 by 1971. Others include Merck, Sharp and Dohme, Bendix, Ametek, Head Ski & Sports Wear, Inc., Hittman Associates, Tristate Electric Supply Company, Optic Sciences, Inc. McCullough Ceramic Corporation, and Chemical Milling Corporation. In addition, General Electric has optioned an 1,100-acre site in and adjacent to Columbia for the construction of a major appliance manufacturing park expected to employ 12,000 by 1977.

A four-year liberal arts college named for Dag Hammerskjold, the late secretary general of the United Nations, will locate in Columbia. The college expects to enroll its first students in 1970. And a community college, to open in the fall of 1970, began construction in early 1969 on a site adjacent to Columbia's downtown.

Litchfield Park, Arizona

In World War I, when German U-boats threatened to cut off the supply of Egyptian long staple cotton needed for truck tires, Goodyear Tire and Rubber Company began growing some on 12,000 acres of land 18 miles west of then-small Phoenix. Some of the land is still farmed, but Goodyear has committed the rest to a new town. In 15 years or so, Goodyear expects that Litchfield Park will boast a population of 100,000 people.

A master plan laid out by Gruen Associates has led to the construction of attractive homes and apartments. A network of bicycle and walking paths lace the residential area to shops in the first of 12 planned villages.

Although the plan calls for industry, one of the biggest businesses may be education. Goodyear donated a 525-acre site within the town to Arizona State University, which will open a branch there in 1970, with plans for an eventual enrollment of 15,000.

Lake Havasu City, Arizona

The building of Parker Dam on the Colorado River in 1938 created 100-square-mile Lake Havasu, but until recently it remained far from the beaten path – 235 air miles east of Los Angeles and 150 air miles northwest of Phoenix. Consequently, many eyebrows rose when industrialist Robert P. McCulloch and C. V. Wood, Jr., designer and master planner, announced plans to turn the mesquite-covered plain sloping toward Havasu into a new town.

They had to house construction workers in barracks and feed them mess-hall style. But the gamble paid off. Today, Lake Havasu is a city of hotels, restaurants, hundreds of homes, miles of boulevards, light industry, a busy downtown commercial area, and recreational facilities attracting hundreds of thousands of vacationists and sports-minded visitors annually. The city's 26-square-mile, mountain-surrounded site is planned for a projected population of at least 60,000, with a quarter of its area set aside for parks and greenbelt.

More than 125 businesses operate and more than a dozen construction firms work to add new homes and apartments. In 1968 there were 1,000 dwelling units in the city, and the population totaled nearly 4,000.

Irvine Ranch, California

Irvine Ranch's 83,000 acres make it the biggest in land area of all the new towns — five times larger than Manhattan Island. The master plan for its development stretches over half a century. Since 1960, more than 190 companies have located in Irvine's industrial complex, and more are on their way. Almost 15,000 persons now live in the Ranch's 11 residential communities.

Irvine also enjoys debt-free land, which few other new towns possess. The ranch was put together a century ago, and Irvine Company has kept it nearly intact ever since. The decision to divert the ranch to new-town development was accelerated by higher property taxes as Southern California land appreciated. The ranch takes up 20 per cent of the land in Orange County, and is 35 miles south of Los Angeles.

Reston, Virginia

Robert E. Simon, Jr., whose initials form the first syllable of Reston's name, conceived and developed this town which has probably received more publicity than any other. Planners and architects have generally praised it since construction began in

1964, but potential home buyers proved slow in coming to the town because of tight money, a price range which initially was limited, and the bold architecture which disquieted some people.

In late 1967, Gulf Oil Corporation took control of the 7,400-acre Reston, and it has made progress by widening the choice in price and design. The outlook is also improved by plans of the U. S. Geological Survey to build offices requiring 2,400 employees on an 85-acre Reston site acquired by the government.

Other New Towns

Near Reston, U. S. Steel Corporation backs *Sterling Park*, whose goal is 3,500 homes, 2,000 town houses and apartment units, plus commercial and industrial areas.

Another new town is *Valencia* in California, being developed by the California Land Company 30 miles northwest of downtown Los Angeles for an eventual population of 200,000. *Foster City* near San Francisco, is planning for a population of 35,000. *Laguna Niguel* in Orange County, California, is rebounding after several years in the doldrums. *Seven Hills North*, nine miles north of downtown Kansas City, Missouri, is where the Norfolk and Western Railway is a partner in developing 1,200 acres.

At *Coral Springs*, Florida, Westinghouse Electric took over the management and marketing staff of a leading south Florida development firm. R. Wayne Nelson, Westinghouse's urban planning director, said the company moved into this field to provide a full-scale "urban laboratory" for testing its skills and products.

> We simply can't permit the past to become prologue. We must build new cities in a better image, making careful use of our land, combining beauty with utility. And despite the obstacles, we must rebuild the old cities to restore them to a new kind of greatness.

Like others, Westinghouse is actively involved in new and old cities. It has formed a subsidiary, headquartered in Washington, "to develop, build and sell low-income housing under federally supported programs and to build, rehabilitate, operate or manage urban projects."

Cities within Cities

Accompanying the trend toward new towns is another to build
new cities within existing urban centers. *New Orleans East* until
recently was a 50-square-mile tract of tidal swampland, largely
undeveloped, within the corporate limits of New Orleans. Levees
are being built and home buyers and industry are moving in.

In Pittsburgh, Alcoa is rebuilding the dilapidated north side into
Allegheny Center, a complex of stores, offices, apartments, and
town houses. In West Los Angeles, Alcoa is putting together
Century City on land which was once a movie lot. An 88-acre
business district holds office buildings, shops, restaurants, and a
hotel. Four high-rise apartment buildings are already in place, and
eventually 12,000 people will live in the development.

Savin Brothers, Inc., Bloomfield, Connecticut, plans to turn 400
acres, six miles from downtown Hartford, into a residential,
commercial, and industrial community called *Parkcentre*.

Although they don't fit the total definition of new towns or
cities within cities, hundreds of major developments meeting some
of the criteria are emerging. Palm Beach Heights Development and
Sales Corporation is building *Rotunda*, a recreation-oriented
community of more than 5,000 acres 18 miles northwest of West
Palm Beach, Florida. Encircling its central core of buildings will be
homes, waterways, and eight golf courses.

Levitt & Sons has begun *Belair Village*, just northeast of
Washington. Adjacent to a larger residential development Levitt
has already built, Belair will cluster seven neighborhoods around a
downtown commercial area. The project lacks an industrial base,
however.

Rehabilitation Projects

Although all the projects mentioned thus far are fundamentally
real-estate propositions, others take a different approach. In 1967
industry helped set in motion a massive rehabilitation plan for the
Bedford-Stuyvesant area in Brooklyn, now reflected in two
parallel organizations: Bedford-Stuyvesant Restoration Corporation, which brings together some 25 grass-roots community

leaders, and Bedford-Stuyvesant Development and Services Corporation, which includes on its board such men as Thomas J. Watson, Jr., of IBM, William S. Paley of CBS, Andre Meyer of Lazard Freres & Company, and C. Douglas Dillon, former secretary of the Treasury.

Working together, these groups have been taking steps toward realizing one of the most ambitious neighborhood-improvement efforts in the country. Long-range plans include more jobs, more and better housing, upgraded health and educational facilities, a community college, a new cultural complex, and two superblocks designed to replace debris and decay with grassy recreational areas.

By the end of 1968, Bedford Stuyvesant had approved 27 ventures with a total financing of $3.9 million, providing job training and employment opportunities for 1,300 individuals. Another 53 proposals were in various pending stages — contract pending, completed proposal under review, or in preparation and under investigation. The 17 with pending contracts or completed proposals under review represented financing at more than $1,240,000, with a job potential of 375.

The approved projects range from retail stores, to franchise operations, to construction firms, to trucking organizations, to manufacturing firms. The largest project approved was for $1.2 million with IBM which has leased an old warehouse in the center of the area for conversion into a cable-producing plant that will employ 300. IBM's is the only approved venture which will not be owned by minority-group interests.

Clean Air, Pure Water, and Quiet

The public today expects industry to play a large role in the solution of environmental health problems ranging from air and water pollution to noise.

Representative Emilio Q. Daddario of Connecticut, chairman of the House Subcommittee on Science, Research and Development, said:

> Past antipollution legislation, as it has been implemented, has raised more questions than it has answered.

He pointed out that pollution-control programs are the responsibility of dozens of executive branch agencies in the federal government and are further fragmented in the Congressional committee structure.

Because of jurisdictional problems, Mr. Daddario said:

> We have a monumental task ahead just to coordinate the technology of pollution control.

John T. Middleton, director of the National Center for Air Pollution Control, U. S. Public Health Service, declared that:

> Efforts of industry and government at all levels to control air pollution have been judged inadequate by Congress and by the public . . . . The public will turn a deaf ear to the old pleas that we must suffer the effects of pollution because we are too unsophisticated, technically, to conduct our business without reducing it.

Senator J. Caleb Boggs of Delaware, a member of the Senate Air and Water Pollution Subcommittee, said:

> Pollution control has become an urgency in the past decade. We no longer have the luxury of awaiting a consensus on the best course of action. We have to act quickly, in the best way we know.

Du Pont's vice president, Samuel Lenher, echoed the sentiment of many in industry when he said:

> Pollution of our environment finds itself not only in our daily news, but with unfortunate frequency in our eyes, lungs and drinking water. Reports of bad tastes in water, smokey and irritating air, and fish killed in rivers are heard all too often across the country.

> Awareness is a necessary prelude to effective action. Certainly we are now very much aware of what ails us, even though we lack magic solutions. Our nation's attitude about pollution has changed from apathy to anxiety.

> We must set quality standards (for air and water) that realistically take into account our present knowledge and establish a reasonable

timetable for industry, municipalities and others to meet those standards. We must develop a broad, nationwide program of research and development to attack problems that are currently beyond our ability to solve. We must embark on a new era of cooperation among governmental agencies at all levels, industries large and small and the nation's research institutions.

Our task is to ensure that every American can thrive in an attractive and healthy environment. If we are going to get on with this job, we must devote our energies to finding answers, not scapegoats.

Unlike the old melodrama, pollution provides no single, easily identifiable villain who can be dispatched with a single shot . . . . In a few cases, it is possible to identify and censure a particular culprit. But in its broadest dimensions, pollution is a by-product of industrial civilization.

All these problems of environment are difficult. The next chapter shows how your company or you as an individual can contribute toward solutions.

The Environmental Payoff

To paraphrase Mark Twain: Everyone talks about the environment; few do anything about it.

At a two-day conference on the subject in Williamstown, Massachusetts, in October, 1968, *The New York Times* reported on October 28 that "two days proved only long enough to nibble around the edges."

The President's Council on Recreation and Natural Beauty sent a voluminous report to the White House in late 1968 on improving the nation's environment. The major recommendations proved less than earth-shaking:

• Federal, state, and city governments should encourage properly designed new towns and cities.

• Federal authority must help the states prevent damage from surface mining and restore past damage.

• Federal, state, and city research and education programs are needed on environmental conservation.

• A study should be made on how to provide more effective tax incentives – state, city, and federal – for environmental improvement.

• The operation of all pollution-control efforts should become integral parts of regional programs.

The emphasis in the report fell on the role of government in environmental control, and government undoubtedly has the prime responsibility here. Yet business and industry can play a part, too. But there is one high hurdle: The economic return on the large investment generally needed to better the environment proves so uncertain that usually only government or large corporations can afford to risk undertaking significant projects.

Money and Housing

Housing Costs — A Key Problem

With present taxation and financing practices, few projects to rehabilitate existing housing or build new housing in the core cities hold much potential for profit. Although there have been profitable rehabilitation programs — Mount Adams in Cincinnati and Bolton Hill in Baltimore, for instance — the rise in rent creates middle-class enclaves. This problem could be lessened if costly taxation and financing practices could be changed. The Housing and Urban Development Act of 1968, with its provision for a National Housing Corporation (Chapter 11), may provide the financing and cut the Gordian knot of red tape strangling ghetto housing renewal now. (At this writing, it's too early to tell.)

If construction could be speeded, financing and labor charges would drop dramatically, and an overwhelming need would turn into an attractive market. Merely replacing the substandard housing in cities would involve more new construction than the total volume of housing starts over the past five years. The 1960 housing census revealed more than 4 million completely dilapidated urban dwelling units, 3 million more badly deteriorated, and another 2 million with serious code violations or dangerous overcrowding. (Recent census studies indicate that the 1960 figures may have underestimated the number of dilapidated units by as much as one-third.)

The key problem is the gap between what housing costs and what low-income families can pay. New housing in multifamily buildings — the kind needed in most city slums — costs from $17,000 to $22,000 a unit, even with an urban-renewal land write-down. Rehabilitated housing, in any volume and in the densities needed, usually costs at least as much. This means that the monthly rent for a $20,000 unit with one bedroom would be about $150. Yet half the low-income families in the slums can afford only $65 to $110 a month, and the other half can afford only $35 to $60 per month.

Until passage of the 1968 Housing Act, government programs to fill the gap had been too small, underfinanced, and overcompli- cated. A fundamental weakness in the Federal Housing Adminis- tration, under whose aegis many programs came until 1968 is that it was never designed for low-income housing. Congress established it in the 1930's to get money moving again and from the beginning built into it the requirement that mortgage insurance be placed only on economically sound properties. Since neither FHA nor practically anyone else can argue that slum areas are economically sound, they almost automatically got ruled out for years, until fairly recently when the public (and Congress) began to favor the idea of more government-supported housing.

Fortunately, banks and other financing institutions have loose- ned up on urban renewal in the last few years, along with the easing in federal attitudes. Some 159 life-insurance companies, controlling nearly 90 per cent of the $170 billion in assets in that field, have put up $1 billion to finance slum rehabilitation. About 90 per cent of their mortgage commitments are insured by the FHA.

Cooperative banking techniques have also proved effective. Five Cleveland banks – Central National, Cleveland Trust, National City, Society National, and Union Commerce – have formed a nonprofit corporation to help finance and expedite urban rehabili- tation. After completion of a project, the mortgage and property are turned over to a nonprofit housing corporation, formed by a church or civic group in the area of the renovation. The corporation seeks federal rent supplements for the tenants. Under such supplements, families pay 25 per cent of their income for rent. The cost above that is paid by a government subsidy.

Large banks are beginning to finance slum housing on their own. Bank of America has allocated $100 million in real-estate loans for home building in areas classified by the FHA as riot-prone and blighted.

On the construction side of slum rehabilitation, only a few companies have begun large-scale projects. One is United States Gypsum Company, among the first of major corporations to do so and leading the way for a number of others.

Some Conclusions on Rehabilitation Projects

U. S. Gypsum officials have learned valuable lessons from projects in New York City, Cleveland, and Chicago. It has similar programs in the works in Detroit, East St. Louis, and San Francisco. Some of the conclusions U. S. Gypsum officials have drawn include:

• The projects will show a profit, besides helping to solve an urban problem.
• Opportunities to develop new products are being created.
• Labor unions cooperate (the company uses all-union labor), but the work needs a better supply of skilled manpower.
• Modernization of a few buildings can improve a whole neighborhood.
• Tenant education — teaching slum dwellers how to maintain their apartments, how to use such ordinary conveniences as bathtubs and telephones — is a necessity.

One reason U. S. Gypsum entered the business was to get other firms interested. Warren J. Obey, project manager, says:

> When you start in the home, you start in the right place. If you have decent housing, then you can train and educate.

In addition, U. S. Gypsum is taking to heart the caustic comment about the home-building industry made by the Housing Guidance Council: "It is very quaint of the nation's largest industry to continue its dependence on 'found' markets while other people get rich on markets that they have created."

What's more, the company uses the projects to develop and prove new products. Two hold exceptional promise — a lightweight gypsum material used to level old floors and a prefabricated dry-wall partition system.

Building for the Low-Income Families

New housing for low and middle-income families has been built in the inner city. A prime example: St. Louis' LaClede Town. Two private companies — Millstone Construction Company, which manages the project, and Renewal and Development Corporation, headed by Representative James Scheuer (Dem., N. Y.) who has been active in housing both as a legislator and builder — made use of Section 221-D (3) of the Housing Act of 1961 which offers low-cost financing as a lure for private companies prepared to accept a limited profit.

Not many private firms like D (3) because it requires them to stay inside rigid cost and rental limits and to be content with no more than a 6 per cent profit on their investment and a management fee subject to negotiation.

For its part, FHA will commit the Federal National Mortgage Association to supply money at 3 per cent — far below the current market — for up to 90 per cent of the cost for limited-dividend corporations, with 40 years to pay.

Besides FHA financing, LaClede Town got a 25-year drop on local taxes and a substantial write-down on the cost of the site, as provided under the Missouri Urban Renewal Act.

The LaClede project was designed for varied roof lines and facades. The houses face courtyards and private streets, with commercial facilities nearby — including an English-style pub.

The key to success in LaClede Town, says I. E. Millstone of the company that built it, is a realistic architect, tightly controlled construction costs, sustained management for the completed project — including a tight rein on collecting rents and such costs as redecorating and maintenance.

LaClede Town has successfully appealed to moderate-income people — both white and black. But Mr. Millstone says he has not earned his 6 per cent return, and he joins the chorus of many builders in calling the limited management fee "unrealistic."

Despite — or perhaps because of — the low earnings, he built a second and larger section of the project, making it possible to spread some of the overhead more widely.

Not every company engaged in slum rehabilitation is a construction or investment firm. Action-Housing, a private organization created by local Pittsburgh business and civic leaders, acquired and renovated 22 rundown, single-family dwellings. It spent about $4,000 for each house and another $6,000 apiece for remodeling and now rents the houses for only slightly more than the rents charged when the houses were slum units.

Encouraged by its initial success, Action-Housing created Allegheny Housing Rehabilitation Corporation (AHRCO) which plans to buy, repair, and sell (for a limited profit) some 1,000 run-down housing units a year. The corporation is financed from the sale of $2.5 million in stock and debentures to 41 major companies, including Allegheny Ludlum Steel Corporation; Alcoa; H. J. Heinz Company; Sears, Roebuck; and U. S. Steel.

Other companies interested in rehabilitation projects:

• Eastern Gas and Fuel Associates has participated in several major projects in the Boston area.

• In a decaying part of Philadelphia adjacent to its headquarters, Smith, Kline and French, the pharmaceutical company, has taken on several projects to help upgrade the neighborhood. The company agreed to pay 40 per cent of the developer's interest charges in renovating 70 vacant houses to make them modern quarters for some 200 low-income families. The buildings are sold to the local public-housing authority and rented to the families, often at lower rents than they had paid previously.

• Cleveland's Warner and Swasey Company, the machine tool and metalworking concern, bought and cleaned up a 40-year-old apartment building in the "tough Hough" area of the city. President James C. Hodge said:

> We believe that private enterprise can and should undertake creative civic development projects where its interests are involved and where it can act in accordance with sound business principles. More than 300 of our skilled people live in parts of the city threatened by decay. With our employees we face all of the problems that come when good

neighborhoods turn into slums. I hope other companies who face the same problems will undertake similar projects.

The company planned eventually to turn the building over to a nonprofit organization.

One program which could lead to rehabilitation largely by ghetto residents themselves is "adopt-a-block" aid for slums. Block Communities, Inc., an agency financed by about $500,000 in New York City money, seeks companies that will "adopt" a block in New York ghettos. Aid provided by the foster "parent" includes help to tenants to secure mortgage money to buy and renovate their own dwellings.

In summary, to rehabilitate or build new housing in the inner city:

• You need not be in the construction or investment business, but you do need to follow sound business principles.

• You must learn to work with government bodies at many levels because government will probably become involved in many aspects of the project – financing, taxes, codes, to name the more common.

• You need to use imagination and creativity to put together a financing-construction-tax-rental (or purchase) package that will meet low-income family needs.

• You must secure the services of a realistic architect.

• You must assure that construction costs are closely controlled.

• You must make provisions for close and sustained management once the project is completed.

• You must teach tenants how to use effectively the new or renovated facilities.

The Challenge of the New Cities

What's the role of the private sector in the development of new cities? Edgardo Contini, partner in the urban-planning firm of Gruen Associates, Los Angeles, answered this way (in the *Center Magazine* for October-November 1967):

The scale of the new-cities program is too overwhelming for private initiative. Its purposes and implication are too relevant to the country's future to be sacrificed to the profit motive alone. Nor should the venture be undertaken entirely by government. Not only would this represent a departure from the nation's tradition, it would deprive the undertaking of the contribution of ingenuity, motivation and capability that private enterprise can provide. Through a joint venture involving the coordinated participation of three principals – government, industry in general, and the building and urban development industry in particular – the program can be carried out. The government should formulate the program and provide the financial support or guarantees necessary to generate incentive. The role of (general) industry should be to develop research and production facilities to establish employment possibilities for the new community. The building and development industry should have responsibility for translating the program into reality.

How can government most effectively participate? Dr. Athelstan Spilhaus of Philadelphia's Franklin Institute and head of the Experimental Cities Steering Committee, has proposed one solution: Form a Comsat-like corporation for new cities, much like the housing "Comsat" already established. Such a government-industry organization would, claims Dr. Spilhaus, create hundreds of small experimental cities across the U. S. He hopes that the first such city will be built in northern Minnesota. The Steering Committee has already collected funds from several federal agencies, plus ten Minnesota companies.

As of late 1968, private enterprise was involved in some way in the building of more than 60 new cities in various stages of development in the U. S. These are some of the major areas for opportunity for business and industry in new cities:

• Technological improvements in the shelter itself. Mr. Contini says:

If the technology employed for the production of appliances, automobiles or farm products was applied to housing, within a few years we could bring unsubsidized housing within the reach of everyone.

Major needs include new materials, new mass production techniques, better methods of site preparation.

• Technological improvements beyond the efficient building
of shelter. For example, industry should explore more fully the
possibility of total climate control. The covered air-conditioned
pedestrian areas of recent years are only modest forerunners of the
potentials already technologically available. Through them, regions
previously bypassed because of climate can be opened to urban
settlement. Opportunities also abound to find new approaches to
water supply and disposal, new techniques of power generation
and distribution, and new methods of communication.

• Transportation. One of the most promising innovations in
the new cities should be in transportation. The building of a new
city offers an unparalleled opportunity to retain the benefits of
private mobility without sacrificing the characteristics of com-
pactness, efficiency, and variety that are so necessary in new urban
areas. A system of private and public transportation designed to
maximize the benefits of both and new techniques of rapid mass
transit should be developed as integral elements.

Three fundamental problems hamper the start of most new-city
plans — financing; assembling the land, particularly when it's near
a major metropolitan area; and zoning, again especially when near
a metropolitan complex. When the Rouse Company began
developing Columbia, Maryland, it was well aware of these three
problems, but it solved them all. How? By incredibly detailed and
complete planning, including consultation with people expert in
such disparate disciplines as psychiatry, psychology, communication, recreation, city management, education, religion, and social
sciences.

Moral: If you want your company to participate in the
burgeoning new cities, you need to plan carefully, too. The market
is tremendous — the construction of a second America in the next
30 years.

The Perils — and Promise — of Pollution

We have grown so accustomed to dire forecasts of air pollution
choking us, of water pollution sickening us, and of sound

pollution deafening us that it seems contradictory to claim that pollution has its promising side, too.

But it has. Wall Street analysts predict that the manufacture of pollution-control equipment will be the major growth industry of the 1970's. It's already a $10 billion-a-year business in sales. The volume of equipment to control pollution has risen an estimated 30 per cent annually, 1965 through 1968.

Industry finds some profit from pollution-control expenditures. It has converted waste from smokestacks and streams into useful by-products. Schenley Industries, Inc., transforms distillery and brewery wastes into cattle food.

American Can Company turns spent sulfite liquor into a concentrated product used for purposes ranging from making vanilla to loosening the mud required in oil-well drilling.

United States Steel Corporation, which has invested $200 million on pollution abatement, has a pilot plant at its new chemical facility near Pittsburgh which it hopes will increase the company's ammonia production by about six times.

Yet the perils of pollution undoubtedly outweigh the promise. The main hazard, of course, is that we may indeed choke, sicken, or deafen ourselves to such an extent that the urban environment won't be worth living in. Many psychiatrists and public-health experts agree that urban pollution has contributed significantly to mental illnesses and substantially to respiratory and digestive diseases.

Noise can cause hearing damage ranging from temporary loss to permanent deafness. If noise doesn't lead to deafness, it may result in dilation of the pupil of the eye, contraction of blood vessels, and changing heartbeat and blood pressure. The high level of incessant noise has contributed importantly to discontent in riot-prone areas.

Another pollution peril is its expense. There are as many predictions as there are experts on what it will cost to rid the nation of pollution. One source says it will take 20 years and $212 billion. Another estimates that the job will require 33 years and $275 billion. Whatever the figure, it means big spending by government, business, and individuals — as well as big markets for the companies making abatement equipment.

What To Do about Pollution

What can you or your company do about pollution? Any or all of four courses of action appear feasible.

1. Help Curb Pollution Through Simple, Often Inexpensive Steps

Along with every other man, woman, and child in America, you churn out four to five pounds of refuse everyday. You can assist importantly by not throwing your beer can in the park or lunch wrappers out the car window. And you can instill an abhorrence of litter in your family and friends, too.

Your company can make its antipollution stand clear to employees. Henry A. Thouron, president and chief executive officer of Hercules, Incorporated, tells his people:

> Our objective is to do more than just comply with state and federal air and water pollution regulations. We want to fully carry out our responsibilities for air and water quality control in the communities of which we are a part.

Tenneco Chemical, Inc., takes a similar position. "As employees of a major chemical company, we must exercise in a comprehensive manner our responsibilities as good citizens and good neighbors in this regard [to fight pollution]."

A large industrial user of water in the South spent more than $2 million on removing contaminants from the water before turning it back into the river. The company never publicized this project. "We had been one of the culprits in contaminating the river," recalls the president, "but luckily that had not been widely realized. We thought we would let sleeping dogs lie." Unfortunately, the dogs woke up. During a political campaign, the challenger for a county post got hold of old reports showing pollution levels as they had existed two years previously. He made a political issue of the incumbent official's apparent laxity in curbing water pollution. The company finally bestirred itself to report the remedial steps it had taken, but it was too late.

Moral: Communicate how you stand and what you do about curbing pollution, even if your communication implies short-comings in the past. Everyone in the U. S. has been guilty of pollution to some extent. You will neither shock nor surprise anyone by inferential admissions.

The oil industry, which began working on pollution problems in the late 1920's, issues periodic reports through its American Petroleum Institute on measures taken to curb pollution. Some might argue that reports of the industry's spending a record $382 million on air and water conservation in 1968 — 40 per cent more than in 1966 — constitutes tacit admission that the problem was 40 per cent worse than two years earlier. Yet no one seriously makes such a charge. On the contrary, the API communication receives a decidedly favorable response.

2. Help Curb Pollution by Supporting Sensible Legislation

To try to cope with the situation, governments at all levels have drafted, debated, and enacted legislation, some of it good, some of it harmful. Du Pont's Mr. Lenher points out:

> Let me caution that in our haste to proceed we do not compound our problems with stringent or unworkable laws and regulations which can have an unnecessarily harsh impact on continued industrial growth. Let me repeat, this is a time for action, but there is never a time for panic.

On the other hand, Mr. Lenher emphasizes:

> We in industry would be shortsighted . . . if we did not concede that voluntary action has been inadequate. There is need for technically sound regulations and standards, and these merit our full support.

A medium-sized company was growing and wanted to build another plant in a Southwestern city. Objecting to a local ordinance requiring expensive electronic precipitation equipment for its new boiler room, the company argued that other expensive pollution controls planned for its boiler operation made the electronic precipitation unnecessary. The company lost its case because for two decades it had fought every pollution-control ordinance considered by the city council. It had achieved an indelible reputation for foot-dragging on pollution abatement.

Moral: Don't cry wolf too often. Pick your cases carefully when you oppose legislation. Recognize that some measures deserve your support. Then stand up publicly for them.

Pittsburgh industries invested nearly $500 million between 1941 and 1948 — in antipollution moves that came long before the federal government seriously involved itself in air pollution. Through the National Council for Air and Stream Improvements, the paper, pulp, and paperboard industries studied the problem even before much legislation appeared on the books. The council has advised many federal, state, and municipal agencies, particularly on the scientific aspects of abatement.

Since 1943, the industries have spent more than $8 million on pollution-control facilities and $25 million on research. That this has proved a sound investment is indicated by the fact that the industries would have to ante up perhaps $1 billion at today's costs if they started now.

Indeed, the pollution-control stakes are rising. We have already seen the scope of the oil industry's annual expenditures. Between 1951 and 1967 steel companies invested some $600 million in abatement. The chemical industry has spent more than $500 million on pollution-control equipment and currently spends $65 million annually to operate and maintain it.

3. Seek Sound Technical Solutions

Technology was the paper, pulp, and paperboard industries' fundamental approach. The Soap and Detergent Association, at a research cost of more than $150 million, isolated and did away with an ingredient which caused the "foaming" in streams.

The mammoth problems of cleaning up the water we dirty and desalting seawater are far from solved. State and federal governments will probably pay industry $270 million a year by 1977 for research and development alone. Frost and Sullivan, Inc., a New

York market-research organization, predicts we'll spend $66.3 billion on water and waste-water facilities between now and 1980.

More and more new equipment appears on the pollution-control scene. New machines and processes are being developed to handle problems few recognized even a decade ago. Examples:

• Weyerhaeuser Company, the big lumber company, has built the first flowing-stream experimental station in the world to study how to manage the quality of water.

• Seven steel producers teamed up at a cost of $500,000 to test the efficiency of a new process in Niles, Ohio, for the disposal of steel wastes.

• The growing practice of sanitary landfilling has evolved as the most satisfactory method for disposing of solid waste on the ground. Furthermore, the practice often takes worthless land and makes it usable for parks, highways, or even for tax-yielding commercial uses.

• Japanese engineers have developed a giant press that reduces volume by 90 per cent for crushing garbage into bales.

• A British firm has developed a jackhammer both quieter and less expensive than most conventional models.

• Dover Stamping Company has produced a sound-deadened galvanized steel garbage can to eliminate the early morning clanks.

• Sinclair Refining Company since 1954 has had a mobile laboratory at Houston which constantly checks the air and water for impurities.

• Wellman-Lord, Inc., a licensor to the Bechtel Corporation, has come up with a process that will eliminate the sulfur dioxide from stack gases at electric-generating plants and turn a profit as well by producing commercially salable anhydrous liquid sulfur dioxide.

4. Lend Your Manpower To Help Curb Pollution

Mr. Lenher of Du Pont states:

I would urge that careful attention be given to all requests from government officials for manpower assistance. The question is not whether personnel can be spared for this important work, but whether we can afford to decline the offer. Industry has often wished to be involved in government decision-making that affects its operations. Never has there been a better opportunity or a clearer obligation.

Battelle Memorial Institute, as technical advisor to the Ohio Water Development Authority which seeks a massive cleanup of the lower Cuyahoga River running through Cleveland, relies on industrial know-how in formulating programs. The project may serve as a new model for industry-community cooperation.

The environmental problems hold both peril and promise to industry. By enlarging on the promise, business can reduce the peril.

13 Aiding Local Government

Adjacent to General Electric's jet-engine plant in Evendale, Ohio (near Cincinnati), lies Lincoln Heights, an all-Negro city of about 8,000. Being primarily residential, it lacks an adequate tax base to support the variety of services needed by a city of that size.

Evendale management has helped Lincoln Heights improve itself. Some of the actions taken include:

• A Joint Planning Committee has been formed. This committee brings a broad range of community interests together with area industry, the University of Cincinnati, and county and state service organizations. The committee identifies critical programs and plans and directs action.

• Considerable attention has gone to helping the schools improve. GE property was transferred to the Lincoln Heights School District to provide a higher tax base.

• The company encourages GE employees who live in Lincoln Heights to participate in city affairs. Two past mayors are General Electric employees; the city solicitor was a GE employee. Management granted another GE employee a leave of absence to become the director of urban renewal.

• GE people helped the community start up a small community newspaper, the first in its history.

• The medical director in the Evendale plant counseled Lincoln Heights people on setting up a medical clinic in the community.

Lincoln Heights isn't the only local community that needs help. Virtually every one in the U. S. can use assistance in one form or another. Business and industry can often provide it – but not enough do. The reason may be explained in terms of what Aaron J. Gellman, vice president of planning of the Budd Company, calls an institution's Innovation Quotient (IQ) – its propensity to innovate.

Mr. Gellman believes that corporate vendors with high IQ's prefer to deal with the companies with similarly high IQ's. For such companies, working with conservative, low-IQ customers would be expensive, hard, and trying. Apply the Gellman theory to the frustrations of working with the typical bureaucracy of a local community. It becomes clearer why many companies avoid dealing with local government even on a business level, much less on the still more difficult plane of modernizing outmoded government practices and activities.

Yet city administrations almost desperately seek new approaches to their problems. Mayors of such cities as Dallas, St. Louis, and New York – to name only a few among many – now search for ideas from businessmen. Companies can provide help in many ways. Four major areas of assistance are management aid, technological assistance, area development, and support on community issues.

Management Aid

The Lincoln Heights-General Electric program is an example of how a company can offer a business-like approach – take a look at the problem, establish priorities, then try to develop solutions.

A study by the National Industrial Conference Board, based on a survey of 356 businesses, states that the solution for urban problems "demands the attention of all forces in society. To modernize and improve local government, to better the business climate, and to solve community problems . . . companies are working with their governments, pooling individual competences for the common good."

Eighty per cent of the companies that the Conference Board surveyed believe that their already active involvement in urban affairs will increase. No company intends to reduce activity. Of those whose participation will remain constant, most say that they are not equipped to do more or that they will assume a disproportionate role in their community if they expand activities.

Yet the great majority will do more because:

- "The need exists."
- "Industry has the brains, know-how, personnel, finances to do the job . . . ."
- "If disorder increases here, this area will be less attractive to business and residents, and our future here will be adversely affected."
- "As we learn more about the problem and have had experience, I am sure avenues that are not presently known to us will open up to help solve the problem."

Examples of Management Aid

- At the request of a New England mayor, a General Electric team of four finance specialists audited various departments of the city's operations. Their recommendations promise to reduce municipal costs by nearly $400,000 a year.

- When the village of Northbrook, Illinois, sought to recodify its village ordinances, it received a bid of $15,000 from an outside firm. A team from the First National Bank of Chicago and three lawyers successfully completed the task without cost to the community.

- A New York bank provides services to the city in the collection of real-estate taxes and water and sewer rents. The bank also has an officer assigned to work with the city's director of finance.

- Westinghouse's advanced-programs department has assisted Baltimore's Bureau of Building Inspection to improve its data-processing system.

- Atlantic Richfield loaned three executives to subtask forces in California to study the organization of the 18 state colleges, the state transportation services, and the filing and records system of the state.

- New York City makes use of a Management Advisory Council which reviews any and all types of problems brought to it by the deputy mayor. The board chairman of Union Carbide Corporation is head of the advisory council. The council may make on-the-spot proposals for solving a problem or may recommend consulting firms and operations people for complex problems. If the problem covers an area where know-how is needed but not generally available from commercial sources, the council arranges for "loaned executives" from business. In 1968 Union Carbide had two loaned executives working for New York at no expense to the city.

Application of systems engineering to urban problems is getting increasing attention from Washington, city planners, sociologists, and businessmen. In various cities — Baltimore, New York, Dallas, and Los Angeles among them — companies are carrying out projects to see whether they can better handle complex physical and social problems by using the group analytic techniques known as *the systems approach.*

In Cleveland, TRW, Inc., has suggested an approach based on the creation of a public-private organization that would handle long-range planning for a 16-county region in northeastern Ohio. In a study for the Greater Cleveland Growth Association, TRW also recommended the formation of a company to provide areawide demographic data and to supply land-use and economic information for community planning. Financing would come from a consortium. The proposed information service would sell its data to customers involved in local planning and would, in turn, be regulated like a public utility.

The TRW study suggests reassignment of responsibilities among northeastern Ohio's numerous civic groups (70 programs in Cleveland for jobs and job training, for example) working on myriad urban problems. TRW recommends that the Growth Association support ghetto entrepreneurship and that it formulate a master regional plan.

Managing Tax Money in California

Sometimes many businessmen can participate in a single project. For example, more than 200 corporate executives pooled their talents, without cost to the state, in a California government study directed toward educating public officials to spend tax money in a managerial fashion.

A 200-page report left in the hands of Governor Ronald Reagan contained 1,405 recommendations. Through September, 1968, the state had implemented 541 recommendations and rejected 299. The potential annual savings of the implemented recommendations were $129.1 million and the potential one-time savings were $17.1 million. A few of the recommendations are the following.

• The team reviewing the Highway Patrol and the Department of Motor Vehicles recommended that the governor drop plans for a proposed 10-story building. The plan was canceled, saving more than $4 million, plus an annual maintenance cost of $400,000.

• The team discovered that the state was assigning at least 25 per cent more office space to each employee than does industry — 155 square feet against 123 square feet. With the application of industry-efficiency standards, two state office buildings under construction could house more than 3,000 employees instead of 2,138 as originally planned.

• A department issuing thousands of licenses every two years with the same expiration date was asked to stagger the expiration dates to provide for a continuous work load.

• Another department that transferred documents internally with a new manila envelope for each transfer, or 150,000 a year, was advised to switch to "repeated use" envelopes. It then needed only 10,000 "repeat" envelopes a year and saved $4,000.

• Not all recommendations led to dollar savings. The group suggested an increase in spending for the state's mediation and conciliation service because of the increased organization of public employees — teachers, sanitation workers, and others.

Establishing Goals

Business and industry have probably made their greatest contributions to government by helping communities establish long-range goals. One of the best-known of such programs began with the long-range plans of Texas Instruments, Incorporated, of Dallas. This program started as an attempt by the corporation to plot its future direction and how it could effectively use its resources. When Texas Instruments' chairman, J. E. Jonsson, became mayor of Dallas, he brought with him some of the tools that had aided corporate development. He gave the following as a reason for instituting Goals for Dallas:

> To realize a worthwhile destiny, Dallas as a city stood a better chance to succeed, as did the business with which I was so long associated, if it had clearly established and well-understood goals and plans.

The Goals program began with comprehensive examinations of current conditions in Dallas by competent researchers. They studied municipal government, design of the city, health, welfare, transportation, communication, public safety, education at all levels, cultural activity, recreation and entertainment, and the city's economy. Thereafter, a conference of 87 citizens of diverse backgrounds met to draft the Goals for Dallas. Thousands of other Dallas residents attended meetings to review and amend the statements.

Mayor Jonsson says:

> Goal-setting, democratically accomplished, gives clear signals to political and other concerned bodies as to what people need, want, and expect. When [the people] set goals for a city, political support for projects required to solve problems is built in.

Consulting organizations that originally worked primarily for industy and business have begun providing a wide range of services for municipalities, regions, and other public and private groups concerned with planning and administering public programs. An example is Arthur D. Little, Inc., the research, engineering, and management consulting company with headquarters in Cambridge,

Massachusetts. Services include assistance in planning community development and model-cities programs, counseling on financial programs and the adaptation of management techniques to public administration. In addition, research programs related to systems analysis, housing, transportation, or physical problems such as pollution and waste disposal are conducted.

Technological Assistance

City officials aren't aware of the potential that technology affords them. Similarly, businessmen aren't as creative as they might be concerning adaptations of various technologies to urban problems. The time is ripe now for city and business officials to get closer together on technological solutions that may ease the urban crisis.

Transportation

Traffic jams cost America an estimated $5 billion annually, counting lost time and wages, extra fuel consumption, lower tax yields, and vehicle depreciation. Even this does not take into account the sales, salaries, and taxes lost because some people find it too difficult, or even impossible, to travel.

In some areas, public transportation almost doesn't exist, leaving those who cannot afford a car or motorcycle without any transportation. That means unemployment for many who can't reach the jobs.

From the technological standpoint, industry has been more active in this area of the urban crisis than in any other. Activities range from the development of products and systems to service on government transportation advisory boards. Examples of research and development:

• Westinghouse Electric Corporation describes an "innovative rapid transit system based on the use of lightweight automated vehicles operating singly or in trains on a frequent headway." It calls for lower capital and operating expenses than required for conventional systems.

• Lockheed conducted a program of research and development on a monorail.

• Ford's Transportation, Research, and Planning office, in cooperation with a university group, is developing a dual-mode vehicle system combining automobile convenience and transit capacity.

• General Electric is developing equipment for fast-transit trains in urban and suburban areas. For example, GE is providing propulsion systems for the new link between Cleveland's airport and downtown and the New York-Washington high-speed run, as is Westinghouse.

• North American Rockwell has developed an experimental system that would improve air-transport safety by detecting clear-air turbulence.

• A major rubber company offers "Dead-beat," a sound-deadening material now being considered for use by the Massa-chusetts Bay Transportation Authority.

• Representatives from a large airline are working with New York City officials to help solve short-haul transportation diffi-culties by converting airport facilities to accommodate helicopters and V/STOL (vertical/short-range take-off and landing) aircraft.

• A California chemical and defense materials company proposes warehousing and material-handling systems to make large centralized warehouses in urban areas more efficient, speedy, and automatic.

• An electronics company developed a computerized traffic-control system designed to speed substantially the flow of vehicular traffic on New York City streets.

• Raytheon's Transportation Systems unit is developing: a device to measure the separation between cars and the rate of closure for safety applications; a Passing Aid System incorporating sensors buried in the road, a data processor, and a dashboard data-reading unit to inform a driver when it is safe to pass and how much time he has to pass; and a Ramp Merging Control system to assist drivers in safely entering high-speed freeway traffic. Raytheon Education Company manufactures the Drivotrainer System, a computer-assisted driver-training simulator used with wide-screen, color motion pictures of highway and traffic situations.

• North American Rockwell completed a study in 1965 of California's transportation requirements over the next 50 years. The study covered possible future developments, including high-speed ships and tube trains, V/STOL aircraft, trucks and buses that ride on a cushion of air, and automated electronic freeways. The company has also performed a study for the U. S. Department of Housing and Urban Development, identifying those technologies that may help solve urban transportation problems in the period of 1973 to 1980 and estimating how much, if any, additional development may be needed to solve the anticipated difficulties.

Transportation Study Committees

Many companies participate in transportation studies — usually of a specific urban-transit problem. They work with such groups as automobile-club study panels, the Transportation Association of America, Transportation Research Foundation, the Transportation Center at Northwestern University, the Oregon Transportation Association, the Bay Area Rapid Transit District in San Francisco, and HUD's Advisory Committee on Transportation.

Several systems firms participate in a committee co-chaired by General Bernard Schriever (USAF, Ret.) and Dean William Seifert of Massachusetts Institute of Technology. This committee considers problems posed by near-future demands on key airport facilities throughout the country. This includes air-traffic considerations and the problems of handling increasing numbers of passengers on the ground.

Ford Motor and Michigan Bell help with the Detroit Transportation and Land Use Study conducted by the Regional Planning Commission. Ford has contributed half the time of a systems analyst and several hundred dollars a month in computer time. Michigan Bell's assistant building engineer serves on the administrative committee, as well as on the personnel screening sub-committees and the finance subcommittee.

One railroad participates in an experiment to update commuter service. A vehicle manufacturer is testing on the railroad's tracks a "hi-rail," a 50-passenger bus for use on both highways and rails.

Some companies assume limited responsibilities for public transportation. A California company buses residents of Watts to their jobs. A neighboring oil company is studying ways to improve public transportation to and from the area. The Chicago Association of Commerce and Industry is developing a system whereby workers living in the inner city will be transported to jobs which the movement and expansion of industry have created in outlying areas.

Law Enforcement

Opinion polls indicate that crime in the streets is the major domestic concern of American citizens. Businessmen have an additional concern: the responsibility for protecting company personnel and property. In some cases this requires company security forces, but most companies rely on public forces for protection. (Chapters 17 and 18 contain discussion of other facets of this and the related topic of civil disturbance.) The following are examples of how business is helping local and national forces.

• North American Rockwell has outlined a research and development program that would employ systems analysis and engineering to design and implement an advanced crime laboratory. The program would begin with a systematic analysis of the interrelationships between the crime lab and other functional elements of the total criminal justice system, including investigation, arrest, prosecution, and other judicial subsystems. North American Rockwell has demonstrated for the FBI an automated system to read fingerprints rapidly at low cost. It's designed to process 500,000 fingerprints a day.

• Police agencies, with the cooperation of Michigan Bell, now have a system, Law Enforcement Information Network, that ties in 140 teletype locations — in state police posts, police chiefs' offices, and county sheriffs' departments – with a computer at state police headquarters. Police can query the computer for information on wanted criminals, stolen cars, etc. For example, a policeman who has stopped a motorist for a traffic violation but is suspicious of the motorist can call his headquarters to have the computer queried. The system also provides access to the national law-enforcement network.

• General Electric's Electronics Laboratory works with the Syracuse Police Department to combat crime through the application of industrial technology. The police-GE team has scheduled four projects for development which will increase police effectiveness – electronic techniques for protecting isolated property, advanced burglar alarms, television recording and display devices to assist patrol units, and a more effective communication system. Other innovations include the use of high-intensity mercury-vapor street lights to reduce crime (and lower accident rates) and information-use studies and data systems for police departments.

• The systems approach can help prevent crime, too. A western corporation completed a study in 1965 for California that was the "first attempt anywhere in the United States to apply aerospace methods to social problems," in the words of Governor Edmund G. Brown.

After six months of research, the company suggested a five-year plan for revising court procedures, improving methods of predicting crime, changing the state's approach to parole, and for producing a cheaper, more efficient system for dealing with crime. Several months before the outbreak of violence in Watts, the company reported that it could occur there – a prediction which unfortunately was ignored.

Many companies have found ways more managerial than technological to help their local police.

• R. J. Reynolds Tobacco Company has for years assisted in training law-enforcement officers and has served on the Police Pension Fund Board.

• Members of the Southern Pacific Company's own police department have participated in police training schools to help upgrade the standards of the company and the public force.

- Sherwin-Williams' director of industrial relations has partici-
pated as a lecturer in Ohio police schools in cooperation with the
Federal Bureau of Investigation.
- Uniroyal's Los Angeles facility has a representative on the
Police Candidates Board who aids in selecting future police
officers.

- A New York City company helped establish the Police Cadet
Program in cooperation with the city's Police Department and the
Board of Education. The program provides a stipend for the
patrolmen-in-training, and the company gives part-time employ-
ment to remove any financial hardship.
- Many companies with their own security forces have tie-ins
with the public police. For example, Detroit police have Michigan
Bell's 150 radio-equipped vehicles, among many others, enlisted in
Community Radio Watch.
- Utah Copper Division of Kennecott Copper Corporation has
equipped the new city-county gymnasium for the training and
recreation of law-enforcement officers.
- Whirlpool Corporation provided funds to place the Benton
Harbor, Michigan, township police on an around-the-clock basis.
- Pittsburgh's three gas utilities have sponsored TV programs
pointing out the duties, responsibilities, and efficiency of the local
police department.

Public Health

Nonwhite Americans have a relatively poorer chance for good
health, compared to white Americans, than they did a decade ago.
The Urban League says: "In all health areas, the disadvantaged
nonwhite has not been able to participate fully in the expanding
opportunities for health and life available to white Americans."
Industry has produced an array of diagnostic and rehabilitative
tools for the medical profession. Devices and systems, often
spin-off developments of aerospace research, have improved or
soon will improve the diagnosis, treatment, and care of patients.
Some examples of this progress are the following.

• General Electric has established MEDINET, a computer service allocated to meet the specific information-handling needs of the medical community, especially hospitals.

• Lockheed has developed an information system for hospitals.

• North American Rockwell has developed a medical laboratory designed to operate in any climate or terrain. Although intended primarily to support military field units, this type of lab could also be used by groups concerned with the public health of civilian populations.

The laboratory is modular, transportable, and features modern medical equipment and instrumentation. The company is also considering a bioluminescent detection system for use in hospital operating rooms to determine toxic levels of anesthetics. It can also be used to detect leaks around stored toxic chemicals used in industry, to detect pesticides floating from target areas in agricultural spraying, and to detect pollutants in air or water.

• Aetna Life and Casualty is participating with Hartford Hospital and the Department of Health, Education and Welfare in an experiment using computers in electrocardiogram analysis.

Area Development

Fortune lists 254 of the 500 largest U. S. companies as being headquartered in the ten largest American cities. Their capital investments total more than $94 billion. The city is more than just the site for corporate facilities. The city is the source of the work force and market for the output. The corporation's economic future is tied inextricably to the city's future. To assure the economic health of the city, U. S. companies use their own talents and the competence of independent groups for area development.

Approaches to area development vary, but there are three common approaches: One company may plan for an area within a city, several companies may jointly plan for a city, or several companies may jointly plan for a region.

Southern Pacific Company has industrial development plans for Watts and other urban centers. Benjamin F. Biasini, the president, explains the company's plans for Watts:

> [The project] is based on the premise that the removal of substandard housing and the attracting of new industries with job opportunities represents a better long-term approach to the poverty problems than the various welfare-type efforts presently underway. Southern Pacific's long experience in industrial development is a logical basis for initiating such efforts, and substantial staff and study fund commitments have already been made on the initial Watts project.

This program provides for the staged development of an area eventually encompassing several hundred acres. If fully adopted, the plan will represent a pioneering cooperative effort between private industry and government. Federal funding would be needed for such large-scale redevelopment.

Informal committees and groups sometimes tackle development problems. Chicago's Economic and Cultural Development Committee combines business and municipal resources to perform these functions:

1. Finds manufacturing operations in land-clearance areas accessible to the urban resident.
2. Conducts studies to determine where unemployment might be reduced by economic help. This includes an inventory of manufacturing buildings to identify companies that might have to relocate soon, assistance in relocation, and a study of the technological impact on selected industries to determine where job losses might occur and where retraining is needed.
3. Works with owners of a 70-acre tract in the stockyards area, once occupied by packing houses, to site job-producing industry.
4. Tries to get federal agencies to provide help to pockets of urban unemployment.
5. Tries to get government contracts set aside for manufacturers willing to locate in hard-core unemployment areas.
6. Aids manufacturers who have problems that might cause them to move. This aid may include zoning changes to

provide parking, movement of sewer and water lines, and serving as a one-stop clearing house for problems involving city government. Several major corporations have stayed in the Windy City as a result of such efforts.

The Economic Development Council of New York City uses an additional mechanism to help struggling businesses – an "early warning system." Banks and utility companies get word to appropriate city departments when small businesses need help with operational problems.

Many area businessmen contribute their time and resources to the Regional Industrial Development Corporation of Southwestern Pennsylvania. In 1962 the development corporation was reshaped to "seek out new opportunities and to adapt to the forces of change" that were bringing about new materials, processes, techniques, products, and markets. Its aims:

- To preserve and expand job opportunities.
- To improve the labor force.
- To broaden the area's industrial base.
- To provide companies with financial assistance beyond what they could obtain through conventional sources.
- To assist firms needing new facilities.
- To accelerate scientific and technological spin-offs.
- To get the region's total resources working as a unified economic entity.
- To help provide a regional environment conducive to more rapid economic growth.

This Pennsylvania group set up a Scientific and Research Advisory Group and an Industrial Development Fund to further these goals. The research unit helps to identify, evaluate, and advance new ideas, products, and companies. It consists of 12 academic scientists and a coordinator. As of mid-1968, it had:

- Laid the foundation for a rapid-transit industry in the Pittsburgh area.
- Organized the MPC Corporation for handling cooperative research projects by Mellon Institute, University of Pittsburgh, and Carnegie Institute of Technology.

- Created a new company concerned with advanced technologies.
- Stimulated educators and professional societies to create new courses (instrument maintenance, for example) and develop a system of technical high schools with manpower retraining programs.

Specific industrial projects of the development corporation include:

- The 700-acre Industrial Park which in five years attracted 28 companies housed in 22 buildings — an investment of $21 million and an employment of 4,000.
- Risk-loan commitments totaling $13.8 million and made in six years to 75 small, diversified companies, preserving or creating 5,200 jobs.
- Cooperative programs, such as the Silver Lake Industrial Park with the Business and Job Development Corporation.

Many companies contribute people, as well as money to development funds. For example, in 1957 General Electric put an executive from its Owensboro, Kentucky, operation on special assignment for three months to raise $250,000 for the Owensboro-Daviess County Industrial Foundation. Oversubscribed in less than a quarter, the foundation continued to receive the official's attention, as executive director, for ten years, until a full-time director was hired. During this time, two new industries were brought to the area, and a 145-acre industrial park was formed.

Support on Community Issues

Businessmen often participate in independent organizations interested in improving city government. Typical groups include:

- The Greater Philadelphia Movement, which spearheaded the adoption of a new and revised city charter.
- The National Municipal League and the Citizens Conference on State Legislatures, which work to simplify local government structures, improve operations, and upgrade state legislatures.

• The Metropolitan Fund of Detroit, which concentrates in such areas as purchasing, joint use of electronic data-processing equipment, training of middle-management people, and manpower needs.

• The Governmental Research Institute of St. Louis, rendering impartial evaluations of and recommendations for existing government programs — including accounting, auditing, and cost control.

• The Coro Foundation, which provides part-pay, work-study internships for selected college graduates interested in public-service careers.

Many companies also lobby with the electorate on public issues. The Jewel Companies supported, through a cash contribution, the Citizens Bond Commission for a Greater Chicago, an educational program that included newspaper, radio, and television advertising and the preparation and distribution of printed material. The purpose was to inform the Chicago voters of the improvements that a pending bond issue would provide — improvements in alley and street lighting, public transportation, garbage and refuse disposal; sewer-system expansion; and construction of municipal buildings.

Joseph E. Seagram & Sons, Inc., in New York gave similar support of advertising favoring a $2.5-billion state-transportation bond issue in 1967. Atlantic Richfield Company, like many firms, communicates its views on public issues to employees. A railroad did even more than urge its employees to vote to merge the governments of Duval County and the city of Jacksonville in Florida. Two members of its law department served on the Local Government and Study Commission that drafted the proposed charter which the voters approved by a two-to-one margin in 1967.

Michigan Bell Telephone in 1964 found that 188 of its employees held 128 elective and 98 appointive offices around the state (several held multiple posts).

Many companies sponsor political-education and orientation programs for employees. Scott Paper Company has an Employees Political Information Committee, one of whose functions is to bring rival candidates to speak before its employees. Kennecott's

Utah Copper Division sponsors a Governmental Affairs Seminar to familiarize its people with the workings of Utah's government through lectures by key government officers and mock legislative sessions. Western Electric, Ford Motor, Whirlpool, and Republic Steel are a few among many companies which sponsor political-education programs. And many others participate in the U. S. Chamber of Commerce Action Course in Practical Politics.

The next chapter explains some of the practical ways to help your local government solve social problems.

14 How To Work with Local Government

The true function of the city, wrote Aristotle, is to make men happy and secure. These days, few American cities perform that role.

The national crime rate is up 35 per cent since 1960. State and local taxes soared 165 per cent between 1958 and 1968. Traffic congestion worsens, now costing an estimated $1 billion a year. New York perhaps symbolizes the entire urban dilemma. It reels from crisis to crisis. The social glue that binds its disparate groups is weakening. Some people charge that New York's business community, with its national and international preoccupations, pays less attention to the city's affairs than do businessmen in other cities. Others claim that New York City is ungovernable by any man or group of men – that its roiling turmoil has gone past the point of rational control.

Yet progress has been made even in New York City. As we have seen in the previous chapter, businessmen are working effectively with New York City officials. One more example: Businessmen's support and cooperation led in 1968 to the first liberalization of the city's antique building code in 30 years, opening up the possibility for a huge market in new building materials.

Moral: Even in New York, you can work with local government. How is it done? As many methods exist as man's ingenuity can devise, but three stand out – modifying the corporate organization to better deal with urban problems; improving techniques to influence local governments; and spurring true industrial development.

The Corporation Reorganizes for the Urban Crisis

In the past few years, companies in fields ranging from retailing to chemicals to banking have added a new executive to the corporate staff. Titles vary from Manager of Urban Affairs to Vice President for Urban Development. Much of the new man's work is to coordinate programs which the company has already begun. But his job goes beyond the routine of minority-group employment and enters such areas as housing, urban renewal, health and education, and master planning.

National developments — the riots, formation of the National Alliance of Businessmen, and continuing militancy of civil-rights groups — have spurred the organization of urban-affairs departments and the appointment of specialists to head them. In addition, government emphasis on hiring and training the hardcore jobless has put a strain on conventional personnel offices. The new urban-affairs department is evolving as an attempt to meet such pressures more effectively.

Some companies have seized the opportunity to apply their own build-in expertise to urban problems. Radio Corporation of America, for example, has created a systems-development organization which will use the company's systems-engineering talents on social problems. Thomas G. Paterson, a specialist in large-scale information systems, heads the group.

Most companies find their urban-affairs talent inside the corporation. They have also discovered that a professional background in urban matters is not essential. L. J. Haynes, for instance, who is now vice president of public relations at Michigan Bell Telephone, was general marketing manager before his appointment as director of urban affairs. Union Carbide's director of urban affairs, John A. LeVan, was a company lawyer. Bank of America's Marvin E. Cardoza, vice president of personnel relations, shifted from a job in governmental finance. Frank J. Toner, General Electric's manager of equal opportunity-minority relations, moved to that job from a position in employee relations.

Other companies do go outside for expertise. Federated Department Stores, Inc., hired Dennis Durden, an urban-development consultant. As operating vice president—urban affairs, he acts as an additional resource for the corporation's participation in community life, always vital in retailing.

Among his duties: service to Federated's 17 operating divisions as they are involved in renewal, minority-group relations, city and regional planning, special community-development corporations, consumer affairs, and strengthening other programs of local government; service in these same areas for trade associations to which Federated belongs; and service to headquarters' senior management in drafting urban-affairs policy statements and speeches, plus reviewing proposed legislation and contributions.

Periodically, Mr. Durden also offers services to cities where Federated operates. For example, a city may develop a broad renewal action program but want an outsider's advice on its feasibility. Federated's local management gets in touch with Mr. Durden who then can assist the community in evaluating the plan.

But other approaches exist. R. Wayne Nelson joined Westing-house Electric in 1967 as urban planning director after serving as senior city planner for Detroit. His job is much different from Mr. Durden's at Federated. Mr. Nelson spends much of his time consulting with Westinghouse's land-developer customers. Mr. Nelson thinks that the corporate urban planner with government experience has greater respect for "real problems" than have government officials.

RCA's Paterson approaches urban problem-solving with the long view:

> The problems of the 1970's need not be the problems of the 1980's if we do our work now.

His group is designing a mobile, multitest health clinic that will make mass screening possible. It will be specially equipped to spot diseases prevalent in slums.

W. F. Thompson, who was city manager of Oakland, California, is now Dayton Corporation's vice president for environmental sciences. Mr. Thompson, who joined the Minneapolis-based operator of retail stores in 1966, sees himself as a behind-the-scenes prime mover in solving problems ranging from race relations to sewage control.

Most companies confine their urban-affairs activities to conventional fields – usually to minority-group employment and self-help groups. Kaiser Aluminum and Chemical Corporation has made Thomas N. Bowdle, a former FBI agent, director of equal opportunities affairs. He reports directly to the president who describes his major role as that of "catalyst." With a staff of two Negroes and one white, Mr. Bowdle coordinates all Kaiser projects involving minorities.

Bank of America's Cardoza reports directly to the top. As a member of the president's office, Mr. Cardoza isn't likely to see his programs diluted by intermediates. Because he has no staff of his own, Mr. Cardoza draws on various departments for specialized talents.

Most companies have tried – and usually have failed – to put a black in the number one or two urban job in their organization. The failure to find qualified Negroes for the positions is not surprising. Less than 1 per cent of all U. S. urban planners are Negro. The federal government has attempted to encourage the training of black people as city planners. The Urban Department prods cities getting federal aid to use Negro planners wherever and whenever possible. So, most of the relatively few nonwhites in city planning perform for governments.

Although the backgrounds and approaches frequently differ among the new urban-affairs men in business and industry, this position is an indication of the mounting concern shared by more and more of top management. Kaiser Aluminum President, T. J. Ready, Jr., says:

> Equal-employment opportunity is a responsibility to be discharged with the same aggressiveness and creativity that we invoke in the normal conduct of all our other management functions.

In short, even if your company hasn't the size to justify the creation of an urban-affairs office, wisdom dictates that one executive should assume responsibility for this function at least on a part-time basis.

The Corporate Influence on Local Government

Largely because of the IQ (Innovation Quotient) mismatches (discussed in the last chapter), the corporate influence on local government has not been profound — until recently. Many companies have shown little interest in doing business with government, let alone helping to solve government problems. And government officials, more often than not, have reciprocated in kind, issuing dire warnings about the results if industry "dabbles" in welfare or other government matters.

For instance, the Human Resources administrator for New York City, Mitchell Ginsberg, echoed the sentiment of many public officials when he warned at a New York State Welfare Conference in November, 1968, against "the notion that there is something magic about free enterprise" that will enable it to succeed in antipoverty efforts where government programs have not. Such public officials miss the point. Most businessmen simply wish to help by contributing their expertise.

Companies can make better contributions if they first modify their organization so that they can better focus on urban affairs. Effective external actions should follow the internal shifts. The outside activities may take a myriad of forms. We'll probe four of the more common types — lending executives, working through established groups such as the chambers of commerce, participating on *ad hoc* task forces, and selling ideas, products, or services to local government.

Lend Executives

For 20 months, H. E. Cunningham drew his usual salary from Kaiser Aluminum while doing little for the company itself. Carl Odening got his paychecks from Union Carbide although he saw little of his Carbide office for two years. In Syracuse, Dr. James F. Elliot is a frequent visitor to police stations — with the consent and encouragement of his employer, General Electric. All three men are members of a growing volunteer army of corporate executives who help to improve governmental operations.

As the executive director of the Jackson County Improvement Council in West Virginia, Mr. Cunningham attempted to make the area more attractive to industry. Mr. Odening joined Mayor John Lindsay's Management Advisory Council to work on problems such as a cost-accounting system for 22 city hospitals and procedural changes in the retirement and pension system that covers 60 per cent of the city's employees. Dr. Elliot, a physicist, believes that the effectiveness of the Syracuse police department can be improved without additional manpower and without budget increases. He proposed to create special crime-control teams that have full responsibility over crime prevention in specific geographic areas. A one-year test of the idea began in mid-1968.

Your company may not need to lend valuable manpower for extended periods as in these three cases. In a month's study, a chemical company employee revised a technique and modified a paint formula for highway guardrails, thus cutting maintenance costs on that item by one-third. A trucking company lent its dispatching expert to a city sanitation department. In a week, the man had revised the dispatching system to save the municipal authorities two trucks and four men. A restaurant chain provides a dietitian who spends one half-day a week in the kitchens of several small community hospitals in the Dallas-Fort Worth area.

To sum up: You can bring about better practices in government by lending your skilled manpower to work where they have special competence. Sometimes local officials will approach you for help, but more often you will have to take the initiative and make known whom you will lend in what areas of expertise.

Work through Established Groups

Organizations such as the chamber of commerce may serve as the channel for communicating your availability to city officials. Increasingly, chambers or similar groups are taking on urban problems.

The U. S. Chamber of Commerce has launched Forward Thrust, which it calls a "process for mobilizing total community resources." This is a voluntary effort to show the people of a community how to organize for action and to help develop working relationships among groups – government, economic, religious, cultural, labor, civil rights, neighborhood, civic, and others. It is not a governmental mechanism, although its success requires government participation and cooperation. It is not a funding mechanism, although part of its function is to explore ways to pay for solutions. It is a process – a way to help overcome the effects of fragmentation in our urban society, a way to lessen many community problems.

Forward Thrust brings together people and groups in a community to (1) identify mutual objectives; (2) name problems blocking achievement of those objectives; (3) examine available alternatives to solving the problems; (4) establish priorities; and (5) act. This program differs from others in that it encourages participation of all responsible groups and citizens in a community; it recognizes the benefits people gain by involving themselves in urban efforts; it does not create a new super-structure in any community; it encourages action on a broad range of problems; and it is local.

Work with Ad Hoc Groups

The Forward Thrust process can lead to the formation of temporary task forces to tackle specific problems. Businessmen have worked through both established and temporary groups – for example, to help the 43,000 residents in East Cleveland, Ohio, respond to the challenge of urban change. In 1960, the aging suburb of Cleveland had a 2.8 per cent Negro population. By 1968, that proportion had jumped to 38.8 per cent. In 1961 City Manager Grant T. Apthorp said at a Kiwanis Club meeting that the city was changing racially and that services would have to be modified and stepped up. Out of that Kiwanis session grew a number of task forces that eventually led to modernization of street lighting; better enforcement of a housing code; improved garbage and rubbish pickup; and the retention of Arthur D. Little, Inc., the management service in Cambridge, Massachusetts, to design a major program for maintaining a racially integrated city, improving services, and expanding community leadership.

Sell Ideas, Products, Services to Local Government

One approach lies in adapting existing products for public use. For example, motor scooters designed originally for the private market have been adopted by the police. Have you a product that the city can use? In many significant ways, businessmen can sell innovations to the city by continuing to do just what they have always done – to seek new uses of existing products or services. For instance, a firm offering janitorial service for office buildings can do the job as effectively for public as for private structures.

A second approach lies in applying your specialized talents to problems peculiar to government. A systems study sponsored by the President's Commission on Law Enforcement and the Administration of Justice has shown that an effective way to improve the apprehension of criminals is to cut the time spent in getting a patrol car to the scene of the crime. To do this, it's necessary to develop a *hardware* system for locating the patrol car closest to the scene. This is envisioned for the GE-Syracuse project mentioned earlier, but the money for it has not yet materialized.

The study of Syracuse problems has already led to the experiment with a crime-control team, the gathering of detailed crime data which the police did not have previously, and the evaluation of other concepts and new equipment.

A third approach to selling to local government lies in bridging the information gaps. Not understanding specifically what benefits technology may offer, public administrators often do not know what to ask for. They tend to buy what they have always bought. At the same time, businessmen often don't know what the cities really need. The classic example in transportation may be the monorail. Engineers have been so intrigued with this for at least a decade that they have tried to force it as the solution for many *nonproblems*. The monorail is technically feasible, but it has not solved problems of congestion and speed any better than more conventional forms of public transportation.

The information gap also plagues businessmen when they make unrealistic proposals. For instance, they have suggested that motorists pay a toll for the privilege of using city streets. The idea would probably result in markedly less traffic, but markedly greater political controversy.

Yet, ways exist to bridge the gap. General Motors built a huge demand for limited-access highways by exhibiting an elaborate Diorama model of a freeway system at the 1939 World's Fair. Professor Athelstan F. Spilhaus sums up the lesson:

> Urbanites don't know what they want until they see what they might have.

New information – particularly as incorporated in a new product – often generates an idea for an innovation by pointing up previously undefined needs and problems.

Budging the bureaucrats is still another approach to selling local government. Now is the time for business to begin marketing innovations to the cities. Almost all the basic ingredients for success are present. Harassed city officials find themselves nearly desperate for solutions. While many still look at private enterprise with suspicion in welfare and related areas, they will buy – even eagerly – technological solutions to their many other problems. Paradoxically, that's where the danger lies. Although bureaucrats were once too conservative, they now often show themselves overly receptive to instant panaceas. Management must refuse to market *snake oil*. Sumner Myers, director of Techno-Urban Studies for the Institute of Public Administration, says:

> Management . . . must look beyond short-term gains to the long-term social objectives of upgrading the quality of urban life. If it takes this approach, it can be sure of ever broadening and richer markets in the cities.

The Problem of Industrial Development

In 1916, an industrial realtor sang the praises of Newark, New Jersey, with this passage from its brochure: "This is unquestionably the very focus point of the whole industrial universe. It is the marketplace where all the world's goods are bought and sold."

Such language would not sound too archaic in some industrial-development advertisements more than half a century later. Yet, industrial-development concepts must change because the urban

situation, as it remains closely tied to business, cannot remain
mired in concepts of 50 years or more ago.

Following World War II, the term *industrial development* took
on the connotation in North America of "programs to attract
industry," especially manufacturing. Thousands of organizations
across the continent began operations with varying degrees of
sophistication and success.

Richard Preston, executive vice president of the American
Industrial Development Council, Boston, points out:

> *Industrial development* applied not necessarily to the public interest,
> but rather to realize upon the real-estate holdings of private entrepre-
> neurs, railroads, utilities, and the like.

Volumes can be, and have been, written on how to launch a
successful industrial development program. Some programs considered to be successful real-estate developments have not proved
successful community projects.

To measure the true success of industrial development, ask
yourself this question: If a 500-man plant locates at Point A, what
will be the result in terms of jobs, the tax duplicate, added traffic
on the streets, smoke in the air, delays at the supermarket
check-out counter, space in the classroom? And to what extent
will the project contribute to an improvement of life? Too often,
only the factors of jobs and the tax duplicate will figure in the
equation that supposedly measures success.

If you become involved with industrial development in your
area, heed these words by Mr. Preston:

> In essence anything which industrial development does or does not
> do – or does well or does poorly – occasions very considerable
> response in the interlocking spheres of economic, social and political
> development. The investment of capital in the potentials available –
> whether for the development of human or natural resources, for
> technologic or facilities development, or whatever their purpose – is
> the true scope of industrial development . . . .
>
> Regional-planning and development commissions, and programs di-
> rected to economic development for essentially social development

purposes through a wide program of industrial development, are a form of political development . . . .

Manufacturing is *a* target — but not *the* target. The local community is *a* concern — but not *the* sole concern. Programs can no longer be insular. They must be comprehensive.

5 The New Look In Corporate Philanthropy

Foes of corporate philanthropy support their position with two arguments: Let government do it. And, we can't afford it.

Rebuttal: If government should take over, businessmen would be forced to pay higher taxes for what probably would be less effective results than those coming from voluntary contributions. The end of corporate philanthropy would also seriously weaken businessmen's claims as responsible members of society.

Of course, business and industry have long contributed to many philanthropic causes, as pointed out in Chapter 7. More than 90 per cent of all the money given to United Funds comes from corporate-sponsored campaigns. Yet, the traditional fund-raising organizations find that the proportion of the total contributions coming from business and its employees (at least through 1967) has been declining or – at best – holding steady. Although no overall figures exist, it's a reasonable assumption that total corporate giving has risen with expanding sales and essentially unchanged federal corporate income tax provisions regarding contributions.

Why doesn't the corporate money go increasingly to the traditional philanthropic groups? Ralph Lazarus of Federated Department Stores gave a clue when he retired as president of the United Community Fund and Councils of America in 1966:

It is my contention today that we (the United Fund and Community Council movement) have come to the point in our history where we have to change direction . . . to a new approach based on a fresh, broad study of total community needs. Events are moving so fast that we either must make such a shift or get left behind — both by those we are trying to help and by those who are making our help possible. . . . We either help organize the rescue squad for American cities or face the inevitable disillusion of our 32 million contributors, the loss of community confidence, the desertion of its leadership and the decline of the voluntary movement.

The implication is clear: Corporations tie more and more of their contributions to projects promising to relieve the urban crisis. The traditional voluntary fund-raising organizations which don't relate closely to that crisis don't get as much money from business and industry.

As businessmen face up to city problems, they will take many approaches. But numerous companies, particularly the smaller ones, still prefer to work through traditional agencies of philanthropy because they don't have the expertise or the time to appraise worthy projects.

Setting the Ground Rules

You will manage your corporate philanthropy more effectively if you set some ground rules. Here are one company's practices, policies, and procedures for handling requests for contributions. Although this is a large corporation, the guidelines are adaptable for small companies.

I. Statement of Policy

It is the policy of the company to provide financial support to charitable and educational organizations whose activities are consistent with the company's business purposes and are beneficial to employees or the public.

II. Primary Purposes Served by Corporate Contributions

To further the objectives of worthwhile charitable activities which advance the well-being of company employees and community neighbors.

To encourage development through research and inspired, competent teaching; to increase the supply and improve the quality of educated manpower; to further the understanding of the objectives and potentialities of competitive private enterprise.

To advance the public welfare, improve the business environment, and stimulate social progress, particularly in locations near company facilities.

To advance the development and exchange of technical and business information and other knowledge that can increase the ability of the company and of business in general to serve the public.

III. Tax Deductibility

The tax deductibility is always considered in evaluating corporate support.

IV. Discretionary Policy

The general corporate support policy is discretionary as to whether, within authorized limits, financial support will be given.

V. Responsibility of Authorizing Manager

Each authorizing manager is required to develop a suitable support program in response to company, employee, and public interests and is responsible for determining whether each proposed contribution is opportune in light of prevailing business conditions and the financial state of the company.

VI. Internal Source of Corporate Support Funding

Contributions are charged against the operating funds of the component or other organization at which level they are authorized or recommended.

VII. Delegation of Dollar Authority

The president has delegated to executive vice presidents the authority to approve companywide contributions of not more than $25,000 to one organization in a calendar year — and has also granted them the power to redelegate.

VIII. Restrictions Concerning Capital Fund Drives
of Charitable Groups

General managers having area responsibility may authorize a corporate contribution of not more than $1,000 per organization per year to a charitable capital fund drive if there is less than an 100 per cent match of employee contributions.

Community or regional charitable organizations conducting capital fund drives cannot normally receive corporate contributions above that amount unless they are at least fully matched by employee contributions.

Exceptions shall be made only under extraordinary circumstances, and then may be authorized only by the responsible company officer after the president's review. (Board of Directors' authorization is required, whether or not fully matched, if the $25,000 limitation is exceeded.)

IX. Support of Charitable Organizations

Contributions are provided by the company component with the most direct interest in the area of support being asked. This would normally be on the geographical match-up basis.

To insure a companywide approach consistent with policy and established practices, the responsibility for providing advice and counsel on charitable contributions is assigned to the headquarters office.

X. Budgeting

Each component budgets for its own corporate contributions.

The contributions budget is usually allocated for specific organizations.

In addition, the contributions budget usually contains an undesignated amount which can be made available for requests received during the business year. The responsible manager determines whether support is appropriate.

The corporate accounting office prepares a companywide contributions budget — exclusive of those items requiring the specific approval of the Board of Directors.

XI. Reports

Corporate accounting annually issues the "Payments to Organizations" report listing beneficiary organizations, including their memberships and contributions, receiving $500 or more in any one year from the company.

After developing your ground rules, you must still find good answers to three questions:

- How much should you give?
- In what form should you give it?
- To whom should you give it?

How Much Should You Give?

The most significant measure of total corporate contribution is its relationship to earnings before taxes. The Internal Revenue Service reports that for the past 10 years on a countrywide basis the combined support of all firms has ranged between 1.0 and 1.2 per cent of gross profits. Corporate support among major firms tends toward a smaller percentage – from 0.5 to 0.9 per cent. Of course, their total contributions are large.

The five companies in the United States which provided the most dollars to United Appeals in 1966 and 1967 were AT&T, Ford Motor, GE, GM, Sears, and U.S. Steel.

Note that in the guidelines given for the large company it placed a ceiling of $25,000 for any single donation to one recipient in a calendar year, except in unusual circumstances. Only you can determine your limit, but it's a good idea to have one in writing, with enough flexibility to allow for the exceptional case.

Probably the favorite – or most convenient – way of measuring corporate support is on a per-employee basis. However, this often is unfair because the ratio of employees to earnings varies widely. For this reason, we hesitate to report corporate giving on a per-employee basis; but for the record, the median over the past decade has ranged between $20 and $25, according to IRS figures. Of course, contributions per employee come much lower and much higher than the median. In a 1967 study of support in 55 large companies, the lowest per capita contribution by any in the sample was $14.87; the highest, $31.41.

In What Form Should You Give Support?

Money still constitutes the major form in which corporations make their contributions. In addition to the conventional United Fund style of giving, many firms make one-shot contributions. For instance, Bristol-Myers Company gave $40,000 to Operation

Better Block, a summer program designed to aid 100 New York neighborhood groups with $400 grants for each.

More typically, one company joins with other organizations to support a single project. Since 1963, 38 corporations, 23 foundations, 16 individuals, three churches, two government agencies, four colleges, and 107 independent schools have provided nearly $11 million to support A BETTER CHANCE – Independent Schools Talent Search. ABC is a nationwide, non-profit organization providing educational opportunity at independent secondary schools for disadvantaged and minority-group youngsters. The program has placed 1,240 students, of whom 823 were enrolled for academic year 1968-69, while 184 have been graduated with scholarship aid to 102 colleges and universities.

But there's more than money in philanthropy. Some other kind of support may be appropriate for your company. Company stock may serve better than money, especially for capital fund drives in which the recipient need not dispose of the stock for a considerable period. Such gifts may prove much less expensive than money to the donor and more acceptable to the recipient who can expect a rise in the stock's value. More than one American charity has flourished as a result of U.S. industry's general prosperity.

Some companies have donated facilities. For example, General Electric gave an unused warehouse to the Cleveland Board of Education for a factory-school. Or you can lend property or equipment in off-hours.

Some firms donate the time of executives. David Rockefeller of Chase Manhattan Bank, calculates that he devotes an average of 40 per cent of his 60-hour work week to public service. Richard L. Herman, head of an Omaha trucking company, contends that the donation of time is the most effective way a small business can practice philanthropy:

> The small proprietor feels like part of the community. He isn't constantly moving the way many corporation executives are.

A few businessmen, however, question the idea that philanthropic chores should be treated as an integral part of an executive's job. Arnold H. Maremont, president of Maremont Corporation (the Chicago-based auto-parts maker) says:

> Of course, everybody has a real obligation to serve his society — as an individual. But corporations weren't set up to conduct charity drives; this isn't their function.

Yet, most businessmen agree that companies can legitimately lend executives to provide expertise. Fund-raising organizations may lack accounting and computer specialists, for instance, which industry can supply.

Many companies lend, give, or sell their products (at a greatly reduced price) in lieu of other forms of support. Auto companies have long followed the practice of lending — or in some cases giving — their cars for charitable purposes.

Some support includes contributions in several forms. For example, General Electric Foundation presented the Cincinnati School Board with $10,000 to pilot-test at two locations a new high-school curriculum — appliance technology — with instructional material developed by the company. This is an example of the best type of philanthropy — the course helped disadvantaged youth to help themselves; it helped solve a serious skills shortage; and it could have a permanent effect because, once developed, it may be used to train many people and can be transplanted to other cities.

To Whom Should You Give Support?

This question is so important that the next chapter is devoted to it. In general, recipients of corporate support may include:

- Schools, colleges, universities, and scientific institutions.
- Educational associations, funds, and foundations.
- Health, medical, and social welfare organizations.
- Community improvement and cultural organizations.
- Public affairs, public administration, and government organizations.
- Professional, scientific, engineering, and technical groups.

Most companies will allow, but not encourage, contributions to independent health and welfare operating fund drives (Heart, Cancer, etc.); activities in which a significant share goes toward the expense of the function (dinners, benefit performances, charity balls, etc.); cultural purposes; or charities concentrated in communities where they have no plants.

Corporations should not support:

• Political parties or candidates with direct or indirect contributions.

• Propagation of a particular religious faith or creed (but this isn't intended to preclude support of programs or activities conducted for the benefit of the public at large on a nondenominational basis, such as the YMCA, the Salvation Army, religiously owned hospitals, charities, etc.).

• Any cause prohibited by law or considered not to be in accord with court interpretations of the propriety of corporate giving.

Judges, tax specialists, and lawyers have progressed through three phases in their views about corporate contributions. In phase one, they held that almost no gifts were proper. In phase two, they believed that a company was authorized to contribute a reasonable amount of money if the gifts seemed designed to benefit the corporation. Finally, the rulings and decisions evolved to phase three, the current doctrine – corporations may properly support charities which are important to the welfare of the communities where they do business.

In considering to whom you should give support, a question often arises: How should you distribute your support? Your circumstances, your needs, and the needs of the community dictate your answer. The following figures show how the 55 large companies whose philanthropic practices were cited earlier distributed their contributions in 1967.

Education	48%
Community Chest, Red Cross	22
Hospital building funds	8

Other building funds   4
All other (none as much as 4%)   18

It's likely that education also leads the list of recipients for total corporate giving. In a study on business support of education for the disadvantaged, the Conference Board reported: "Education is fast becoming recognized as one of this country's most important products, and business and industry are investing more and more time, money, personnel and creative thought to produce new and better brands of it for those critically needing scholastic services. Companies' motives, as they report them, vary. It may be to raise the quality of living for all of society's members, or to solve pressing urban or community problems or to fill their staff with more soundly qualified people."

The Conference Board found that 90 per cent of 335 firms queried have bolstered educational opportunity for the disadvantaged. The findings do not include data on job training. Questions were intended to deal specifically with what companies do to aid or originate programs of general, basic, or higher education for the disadvantaged.

A special set of questions was given to 93 companies, asking them to indicate the financial support they contribute to national organizations aiding Negro education. Most aid goes to two among about a dozen — 92 per cent supporting the United Negro College Fund and 72 per cent the National Urban League.

16 How To Manage Your Corporate Philanthropy

Aaron Scheinfeld, board chairman for Manpower, Inc., the temporary help organization, makes this charge:

> In recent years, business has enlarged and expanded the scope of its philanthropic activities, and has even supported some government efforts in these directions, but all this has only partially met the needs of the times, and it has not been directed at the most urgent needs.

We can trace many of the failures of corporate support to several major causes:

1. The tendency of many corporate givers to think in terms of personal inclinations and interests, rather than the needs of society. While giving large sums to our alma maters, we may have contributed little or nothing to support school activities for ghetto children.
2. The inertia that plagues all humans. We have contributed for years to this fund-raising effort and that college drive. We may dimly recognize that the charity or school, although pursuing worthy objectives, does not follow goals relevant to the urban crisis. We rationalize our failure to increase philanthropy for the crisis-oriented agencies by saying, "We'll look at that new request next year."

3. The reluctance to become involved. Nobody likes the problems of the city. They are all unpleasant; many are dangerous. We complain about them — but often from the sidelines. Our philanthropy reflects our preference for problems of the Boy Scouts rather than the *unsavory* difficulties facing the Boys Clubs.

4. The failure to see in the alleviation of poverty and slums a frontier for business. Dr. Simon Ramo, vice chairman of TRW, Inc., predicts that the field he calls "public problems" — housing, employment, transportation, pollution, education, and medical care — will absorb more than a trillion dollars between now and 1977.

A New Approach

There are eight general precepts to reconsider in your approach to philanthropy.

1. Keep your corporate giving as local as possible. Few companies have the resources to support more than local programs. You can keep track of the local projects, get more directly involved, and make your contribution visible. More than one company with admirable, broad philanthropic activities has found itself in trouble with local civil-rights groups who wanted local support rather than general support.

2. Confine your support to specific, well-defined purposes. Many government antipoverty programs have failed because they were too general. Don't make the same mistake. A vague project to relieve poverty will almost certainly fail, but a specific program to provide jobs has a good chance of success.

3. Provide support in a form that helps recipients to help themselves. The hand-out may relieve, but it will seldom solve a problem. In a midwestern city, a construction company turned down a request for funds to repair slum homes. Instead, it supplied materials and expert advice to the residents so that they could repair their own dwellings.

4. Make your support relevant. William A. Orme, consultant on corporate support for General Electric, asks:

Is it appropriate, given today's needs and priorities, that the Boy Scouts and the YMCA with their generally middle-class constituencies receive 68 cents per capita from the typical United Fund, while Boys Clubs and Settlement Houses receive but 36 cents? . . . I see little significant change in the allocation "mix" in recent years — despite changing needs.

5. Budget for philanthropy, just as you plan for any other legitimate business expense. That budgeting must be done as you perform your total fiscal planning task — usually plans are made in the fall for the following year. This planning may reveal that you should make a greater investment in total support. It can also show where you can legitimately prune existing programs.

6. Make your corporate contributions pay off. Judge any corporate contribution as an investment made for a measurable return. Such a return could include: benefits to employees and their families; a more favorable attitude by one of your key publics; or a better climate in which to pursue business objectives.

7. Provide more than money. Philanthropy should open new channels for self-betterment for anyone capable of responding to opportunity.

8. Identify, isolate, and attack the 20 per cent of the causes of poverty that account for 80 per cent of the trouble. Statistical specialists have long been familiar with the Law of Pareto which establishes the existence of the 20/80 ratio in most situations. Attack the vital few causes rather than the trivial many. For example, you probably would be wise to contribute to an agency that concentrates on training people for available jobs rather than to contribute to one that emphasizes improvement in the less important areas of grooming, verbal skills, how to conduct a job interview, etc.

Recognize and attack the phychological factors that perpetuate poverty. Resist superficial efforts to relieve it. The psychological factors mainly result from years of conditioning by a hostile or heedless environment. While black Americans bear the major brunt of this condition, many whites also find themselves trapped in repressive or regressive environments. The *lady bountiful* approach to these people won't relieve the psychological ills. But a technique that offers them jobs and hope for the future perhaps will.

Mr. Scheinfeld suggest that you concentrate mainly on poverty in your philanthropy even though other social problems obviously abound.

> I think some of these [other ills] are secondary to the here-and-now problem of poverty . . . and some, such as crime, could be greatly reduced if their underlying cause — poverty — were removed first. To be sure, there can be crime without poverty, but this does not alter the close correlation between the incidence of crime and the incidence of poverty.

Weighing Philanthropic Decisions

Although eight general guidelines can help you measure your broad outlines for corporate giving, you need more specific ground rules in weighing individual philanthropic decisions. Consider these nine questions:

1. Can the fund-raiser offer evidence that his agency effectively identifies new and changing needs and eliminates or reduces out-dated services with no significant disadvantage to the community? Managers of charitable and other fund-raising organizations suffer from inertia just as everyone else does. You can legitimately ask how they overcome the status quo.
2. Is there effective communication and coordination, both at the policy and the operating levels, between the potential recipient and other state and local welfare groups — United Funds, independent non-United Fund agencies, religious-affiliated agencies, *poverty* committees, government planning organizations, minority groups, law enforcement bodies, etc.? Watch out for the agency which feuds. Again, demand evidence of cooperation.
3. Will the canvassing group join others in combined drives? If not, why not? Some legitimate reasons exist for independent campaigns — a capital fund vs. an annual drive, for example

— but examine them carefully. And look twice at all capital fund efforts. Is it truly a capital campaign or a camouflaged secondary annual effort?

4. Does the group make a serious and sustained effort to provide the optimum income from sources other than the annual contributions? For example: For those clients able to pay all or part of the cost of services, does the agency apply a realistic *sliding scale* fee schedule? Does the agency have an endowment which realizes a reasonable annual return? You can and should get answers to such questions.

5. How does the agency establish its campaign goal? Is it based on a demonstrated need or on what the agency officials believe they can raise? Any group should precisely explain the methods it used to set its goal.

6. Is each significant *nonbusiness* group in the community (professional organizations, governmental employees, school, and college people, etc.) providing its fair share of the goal on an equitable basis, compared to business and industry and their employees? Companies and their employees should not be required to give all or substantially all the support.

7. Is there a well-defined, equitable salary and benefit plan for the fund-raiser's professional and nonprofessional employees? Salaries and benefits necessarily take a major share of an agency's operating costs. Accept that fact, but insist that those expenses are fair.

8. When your employees or their families have sought the services of the soliciting agency, has the service been provided in a timely, professional, and useful manner? Here's one of the best ways to gauge the fund-raiser.

9. Has the business community in general — and your company in particular — provided the necessary leadership and assistance to help the agency satisfactorily answer the questions posed here? Further, can you aid if the answers reveal less than acceptable situations? In short, you must do more than just grade the solicitors like a mediocre teacher judging students. Like a good teacher, you want the students to "pass." Like a good teacher, you help them remedy unacceptable situations.

The Art of Saying "No"

Inevitably, you must turn down some requests for support because they don't and can't meet the general and specific guidelines cited or because you lack the required resources. Here are points to emphasize in letters of refusal:

• Your firm is committed already to a substantial corporate support program which it must maintain.

• Deserving requests always far exceed the necessarily limited funds.

• Your support program must be, and is, based on the changing needs and priorities of the business, of employees, of stock owners, and of the community and the public.

• All these factors require you to make difficult decisions continually, frequently causing you to choose from among many desirable programs, organizations, and institutions.

These same points apply when you do not give as much as requested or when you reduce your support from previous years. One other consideration: Sometimes it's better psychologically to give nothing than to give what you or the solicitor consider as inadequate.

When you turn down any petitioner, you must do more than say "No" politely. You must tell what your company does do and why you regretfully cannot expand the limits of the present program to include his cause – despite its deserving nature.

The classic – but not recommended – letter of refusal read in full: "I have nothing but praise for your program."

Special Philanthropic Considerations

We have thus far only touched on one demand for corporate support – capital fund drives – that presents a special problem in the typical community. Now, let's explore what business and industry can do to help bring order to the disorganized campaigns that many nonprofit agencies and institutions wage to finance their capital fund requirements. Although such drives principally involve voluntary hospitals, they also include YMCA's, Boys

Clubs, Community Centers, etc. There are three symptoms of disorganized community campaigns:

• The board and the staff of the agency or institution seeking the capital funds independently determines what it needs, unilaterally establishes a plan, and presents it to the community for support.

• There is a long line of nonprofit groups who appear to be waiting, each one impatient to launch its drive, with one such drive held about every year on a more or less random basis.

• The drives conspicuously lack the kind of broad-based support that has proven so necessary, accepted, and appropriate for campaigns of organizations such as the United Fund or the American Red Cross.

If one or more of these symptoms prevail in your community, the first and most important step is to establish a community leadership group representing contributors. Then charge this body to review for the community each proposed capital fund drive. Businessmen who have done this soon find that the agencies seeking capital funds eagerly vie for the imprimatur of such a group. Sometimes, depending on the community size and frequency of capital drives, your committee may find it expedient to hire a consultant, full or part-time, to appraise the plans and report to the leadership unit.

To attack the second symptom — capital drives from one agency after another year after year — the leadership committee can suggest a planning program to combine drives for all approved agency and institutional needs covering perhaps a three- to five-year period.

A combined drive could usefully and properly be described as the one capital solicitation for the next several years. Its success would eliminate the need for any further capital fund giving for several years. This would allow both the business community and the individual to plan and budget charitable contributions more effectively.

This leads to another special consideration about corporate philanthropy: Should a company require that its corporate contribution be tied in some way to what its employees give?

Firms commonly use a formal or informal formula in determining their support for operating campaigns. Among 40 major contributors, the average is $1 in corporate funds for $2.50 in employee support, but occasionally the ratio goes to $1 for $4.

Although most companies want some matching formula in operating campaigns, few do on capital drives. Yet, the matching idea seems sound for both situations because much philanthropy benefits employees directly or indirectly. A measure of the recipient's effectiveness lies in the degree to which employees will contribute. The few companies that do require matching in capital drives are attempting to persuade other corporate givers to have a similar standard.

Another trend: to persuade more corporations to contribute to capital drives. Presently, some corporations which support operating campaigns generously will not give to capital efforts, largely because a few have turned out to be camouflages for the second annual drive. The true capital campaign, nevertheless, has just as legitimate a claim for corporate support as the operating effort.

The normal practice is to budget the corporate giving on the basis of the determined ratio, at least in the more common operational drives. If employee giving is unexpectedly high or low, the company can adjust its support appropriately the following year. Seldom does the company adjust retroactively. An exception may occur if the employer's employment level changes substantially from the budgeted level.

You can usually accurately determine what employees contribute because more and more do it through payroll deductions, a practice encouraged by the fund-raiser and generally accepted by the employer. Yet, if your employees don't contribute by payroll deductions, ask the agency for the figures. All well-managed agencies keep excellent records on such matters.

One final special consideration concerns the involvement of company executives in charity drives. If you or others in your company serve on campaign boards and committees, don't imagine that such effort absolves you and the company from financial support. Far from it. Such participation is inevitably an implied obligation to provide your own company's financial support and probably to solicit others for theirs.

Some may still say that pervasive government spending for social welfare makes an anachronism of voluntary giving. Actually, the opportunities for effective philanthropy have never been greater. The harsh realities of economics have all levels of government in a bind today. Even Uncle Sam's resources are limited.

As much as any single gauge, your philanthropy measures the conscience of the community. Henry Ford II stated the case when he said:

> We must make it abundantly clear that our national concern for humanity has been imposed by free people upon their government — not by government upon an indifferent people. To that end, voluntary giving speaks with a conviction and a sincerity that tax collections can never command.

17 The Riotous Environment

The law defines a riot as "a disturbance of the public peace by three or more persons acting together in a disrupting and tumultuous manner in carrying out their private purposes."

Even under the more common connotation of the word, "a violent public disorder caused by a group or crowd of persons," civil disturbances are occurring in the U.S. with alarming frequency. Businessmen can understand better how to deal with the riotous environment if they are aware of its historical and sociological perspectives.

Four Questions About Riots

Businessmen should know the answers to four questions involving the how, why, what, and who of disorder.

How Did We Get This Way?

Under either of the preceding definitions, America has suffered many riots. Dr. John P. Spiegel, director of the Lemberg Center for the Study of Violence at Brandeis University in Waltham, Massachusetts, and consultant to the National Commission on the Causes and Prevention of Violence, says that the slum and campus riots of recent years are not a new phenomenon.

As a nation, we suffer from historical amnesia. We have an image of ourselves as quite peace-loving and rational beings. The United States citizen thinks of himself and his country ordinarily as governed by democratic, rational, peace-loving instincts. But the fact of the matter is otherwise. We have always been a violent country, and in our country there have been repeated cycles of violence, cycles of rioting, which we tend to forget about. It is easy to see why this happens, because these particular episodes in our past certainly don't fit into our self-image as being so peace-loving and so rational.

Thus, we have forgotten about Shays' Rebellion of 1786 when a group of hard-pressed farmers in the western part of Massachusetts, resentful about the tax laws passed by their state legislature, seized the law courts and frightened the legislators into modifying the offending laws. Dr. Spiegel says:

[Shays' Rebellion is] a prototype of what has happened ever since with respect to the uses and functions of violence.

We have forgotten about the anti-Catholic riots – the anti-Irish riots – of the 1840's and 1850's, with a particularly bloody outbreak in 1844 in Philadelphia, the City of Brotherly Love.

We have forgotten about the draft riot of 1863, in which 2,000 people were killed in five days. Dr. Spiegel says of the draft riot of 1863:

We have had nothing like that in the current series of urban disorders.

We have forgotten about the anti-Chinese riots in Los Angeles and San Francisco in the 1870's, which were described by Dr. Spiegel as "extraordinarily cruel."

We have forgotten about the labor uprisings, the series of episodes in the course of union attempts to gain bargaining rights. These began seriously in the 1890's and led to such bloody affairs as the Homestead Strike and the Pullman Strike. The nation mobilized as many as 16,000 federal troops to contain those disorders that spread rapidly through the country. Dr. Spiegel reminds us:

Again, we've just had nothing like that in terms of the numbers used for law enforcement in our current series of difficulties.

And finally, most of us have probably forgotten the anti-Negro riots of 1919 and 1920, characterized by whites attacking blacks.

Dr. Spiegel says the present-day urban disorders constitute the seventh major cycle of U. S. riots. And those seven don't account for a lot of minor outbreaks, nearly all of which have affected business and industry in some manner.

Why Riot?

Why do people riot? More specifically, why have the black people been rioting recently? Harvard Professor James Q. Wilson, one of the best informed political scientists in the nation, says of crime and related urban problems:

> Some say that Negroes riot because their lot is deplorable — that they have nothing to lose but their burdens. But the lot of many Negroes has always been deplorable; indeed by most standards it is much less deplorable today than 20 years ago.
>
> Others modify the theory by introducing the notion of relative deprivation or the "revolution of rising expectations." But Negroes have experienced such deprivations and such expectations before — during World War I, World War II, and the Korean War when their incomes rose rapidly, migration to the big cities was heavy and an awareness of and contact with the advantages of white society were widespread. There were no major Negro riots then; the only major riots were begun by whites. . . . The only major Negro riot took place in Harlem in the depths of the Depression (1935), when presumably there was a "revolution of decreasing expectations . . . ."
>
> The few things we know about the riots . . . should lead us to be skeptical of arguments that the riots can be explained entirely or primarily on the grounds of material deprivation, unresponsive local governments, inadequate poverty programs or the like. No doubt these factors play a part . . . . But if class is a necessary explanation, it is not a sufficient one. To material . . . explanations must be added the role of ideas and the role of force . . . .

Theories of social change are often suspect in my eyes because they seem to lead automatically to the policy conclusion favored by the author. . . . If one wants a "Marshall Plan" for Negroes, then economic want causes riots; . . . if one wants Stokely Carmichael and Rap Brown put in jail, then conspirators are the cause. Since no one wants (at least publicly) ideas to be controlled, the causal power of ideas is rarely asserted . . . .

Only a fear of being thought illiberal may prevent us from considering that the probability of a riot is increased by demands for "Black Power," by a constant reiteration that white bigotry and racism are at the root of all the problems besetting the Negro, by the reaffirmation of the (untrue) assumption that most Negroes live wretched lives and that matters are going from bad to worse, by constantly predicting apocalyptic violence if "something isn't done" and by "discovering" the nontruth that all Negroes are alike in their hatred of "whitey" and their tacit or open approval of extreme solutions for their plight.

As Professor Wilson indicates, explanations for riots vary according to who is enumerating the reasons. They also vary sharply according to respondents' race. For example, see Table 17.1 for the 1967 survey showing how whites and blacks differed in appraising the major reasons for riots.

Table 17.1

Major Causes of Riots

According to Whites		According to Blacks
34%	Lack of jobs for young Negroes	67%
37	Lack of firmness by local mayors, governors	24
33	Hatred of whites by Negroes	20
23	Desire of Negroes for violence	13
39	Lack of decent housing for Negroes	68
26	Desire of Negroes to loot stores	9
46	Lack of good education for Negroes	61
8	Police brutality against Negroes	49
30	Lack of progress in giving Negroes equality	72

What Ignites Riots?

Dr. Sol Chaneles of Urban Resources, Inc., in New York City has identified 17 indicators of potential urban violence, based primarily on a study of the mid-1960 riots. He combines the indicators into five clusters:

Cluster I. Predisposition to commit violence as a method for producing change. This cluster comprises three indicators — expressions of the will to commit violent acts; expression of the will to continue violence after the intervention of law enforcement controls; and expression of the will to direct violence against specific targets, such as buildings owned by slum-lords, businesses owned by neighborhood merchants who purportedly *gouge* slum dwellers, and businesses with discriminatory hiring practices.

Cluster II. The existence of violence-readiness factors. This cluster, according to Dr. Chaneles, comprises three indicators — informal training centers to teach riot techniques; illegal movement of small arms into the central city; and the movement of released misdemeanants and felons, both white and black, into urban communities.

Cluster III. Expressions of dissatisfaction with local government. This area includes four indicators — statements to the effect that local government is generally corrupt; expressions of skepticism as to the validity and capability of upgrading programs; widespread rejection of certain upgrading programs as *tokenism*; and expressions of general dissatisfaction about the amount and quality of health services available in poor neighborhoods.

Cluster IV. Government institutions as breeding grounds for violence. This cluster, says Dr. Chaneles, consists of two indicators — expression of dissatisfaction with the juvenile and family courts and verbalizations by both whites and blacks about police-community relationships.

Cluster V. Economic exploitation of the Negro community by the white underworld. This cluster has five factors — tensions generated by Negro succession to positions of control in the underworld and four specific areas of underworld activity which are, by and large, controlled by white criminals but which flourish in Negro neighborhoods. These include the distribution and sale of stolen merchandise; the distribution and sale of drugs; white ownership and patronage of houses of prostitution and allied call-girl operations; and the white domination in Negro neighborhoods of illegal fiduciary operations, such as loansharking, gambling, and policy games.

Dr. Chaneles points out that all or many of the 17 indicators are present in 100 of the largest U. S. cities, presaging the possibility for violence at any time. That doesn't guarantee that disturbances will occur. The indicators are just a warning.

Some signs indicate that many black militants have changed their focus from violence to winning control of communities. They want a voice in the schools (a major objective in New York City, for example), more influence with the police (as in Los Angeles and other cities), more say about what's done with federal aid (particularly emphasized in Chicago), or more political power (achieved in Cleveland).

Roger Wilkins, a respected race-relations specialist with the Ford Foundation, offers hope:

> A lot of white people think that blackness, and black consciousness, means revolution, looting, and burning. But what it really means is what white people have wanted the black people to do for some time — get together to help themselves. If white America sees this movement for what it is, we may be out of the woods as far as mass rioting is concerned.

Not everyone is as sanguine as Mr. Wilkins. Kenneth Clark says:

> Violence is essentially a catharsis. It releases tension that has built up. I don't think the lessening of violence this summer (1968) was because of anything that was done. And without fundamental changes in our society, any incident could trigger new violence.

One final comment on the question of whether this nation has seen the last of the riots: Remember the history of violence in America.

Who Riots?

The National Advisory Commission on Civil Disorders study of riots during 1967 in Cincinnati, Dayton, Detroit, Grand Rapids, Newark, and New Haven exploded three impressions about the people who riot.

The first fallacy is that only a small proportion of the Negro community participates — "probably less than 2 per cent." (In the six cities studied, about 18 per cent of the black residents probably took part.)

The second fallacy is that riffraff — the "outside criminal element" — did most of the damage. (While such people participated, most of the arrests involved young adult Negro males living in the urban ghetto.)

The third fallacy is in assuming that the "majority of the Negro residents opposed the riots." (The commission found an ambivalent attitude by black people toward rioting, but nothing clearcut.)

Some other findings about people who riot:

• Although the rioters who were arrested were male by 9 to 1, more women participated than generally is thought. The police do not arrest females as readily as males. A survey in Detroit estimates that 40 per cent of the participants were women although only 10 per cent of those arrested were female.

• More than two-thirds of those arrested were 18 or older. More juveniles participated, however, than the proportion of those arrested would indicate. Again, the police are less inclined to arrest a youngster than an adult.

• The majority of the rioters were employed. About three-fourths of those arrested had jobs.

• Although from 40 to 90 per cent of those arrested had criminal records, the commission said the criminal element was not over-represented because criminologists estimate that from 50 to 90 per cent of the Negro males in the ghetto have records of arrests. To brand most rioters as criminals, says the commission, "is simply to brand the majority of Negro males in the urban ghettos as criminals."

• "We found," says the commission, "that arsonists and looters were more likely to be older, Southern-born, and employed than assaulters and disorderly persons."

• Among both black men and women, the older the person the less likely he or she was to use violence to gain Negro rights and the less likely would he or she be to join in a riot.

In the Middle of a Riot

What do you do as a businessman when people threaten your plant in a riot? In July, 1967, the people of the Newark Lamp Plant of General Electric faced such a situation – their most traumatic experience since the facility was erected by Thomas Edison in 1905. Through more than 60 years of expansion and development they built a plant that became a prime supplier of incandescent lamps to the eastern United States.

Yet in that time of plant growth, the area around it decayed, becoming one of the nation's large ghettos – the scene for the violence in the summer of 1967 that exacted a toll of more than 20 dead, 1,200 injuries, 1,600 arrests, and millions of dollars in losses from fires and looting.

The riots that began in the New Jersey city on July 12, 1967, came as scarcely a surprise to M. E. (Pat) Patterson, manager of the Lamp Division's facility there. For months, employees had been molested while coming from or going to work and had suffered thefts of their automobiles or parts from their cars. And the plant was frequently vandalized.

In May, June, and early July, Mr. Patterson made several visits to the deputy mayor's office to discuss the problem and to urge civic officials to speed up the availability of land for the plant parking lot. The Newark factory is in a congested area, and most employees had to park their cars on the street. An urban renewal plan included provision for off-street parking for the plant employees but had been delayed.

Of course, no one knew when or even if trouble might start, but additional fire-control equipment had been ordered and installed months before the outbreak. Also, Lexan had been ordered to replace the breakable glass in the windows. The unbreakable and transparent plastic had not arrived at the time of the outbreak, however.

Like tiny sparks that ignite disastrous fires, the incident which started the Newark riot seemed trivial: A Negro taxi driver was arrested on the evening of July 11 for tailgating and brought to the police station a few hundred yards from the lamp plant. There, it was claimed, he suffered from "police brutality."

Throughout the neighborhood, some person or group circulated a crudely printed sheet which called for a protest rally next evening in front of the police station. A crowd assembled and overflowed to the plant gates. A large, 12-story apartment project across the street from the lamp facility and the police station seemed to be the nucleus for the protestors on July 12.

Although the riots raged immediately outside the plant gates, no one got by a beefed-up private guard force. Some employees were stopped by rioters during the early hours of the disturbance on their way to and from the plant, and one employee's car was burned. Other employees were robbed or assaulted.

Mr. Patterson recalls:

> When it became evident that things were getting out of hand, we gave employees the option of going home, although many wanted to work. Later we had to close down completely. (A company station wagon was used to escort groups through the riots, and police escorts were requested.) Snipers were holed up in the apartment building across from us; mobs surged through the streets; and we were being pelted by bricks and rocks.

When most of the people were out of the plant, Mr. Patterson turned his attention to protecting the facility. Besides himself, he had ten defenders, mostly supervisors. Each man was assigned areas to patrol. Fire extinguishers were put where they might be needed. An area that could be barricaded and defended was prepared within the plant. The facility is built around a large courtyard, with two overhead doors at the front closing it to the street. Big supply trucks were moved behind the doors to slow down any possible looters entering the courtyard. Four-inch fire hoses were made ready. Nobody was armed.

Perhaps because of these preparations, no concerted attack on the plant occurred. Mr. Patterson also credits the work of the local union president, Charles Garland, a Negro, who spread the word for days that "there's nothing in that plant but light bulbs."

On July 14 New Jersey State Troopers and National Guardsmen arrived and sealed off the riot area — including the plant. A tank and two truckloads of troops took up positions near the front of the plant.

Who Are Victims of Riots?

Surveys show that destruction may be selective during riots. Violence is not always purely spontaneous. In the 1967 outbreaks, stores which for years had been overcharging residents were destroyed. Those whom customers felt were giving them a fair shake were usually untouched. One example: Sears, Roebuck and Company, in the central area of looting and destruction in the Lawndale section of Chicago, was not damaged. Why? Fifteen years ago, Sears got intentionally and deeply involved in the community and its needs. Its projects include a health center, an educational program for high-school dropouts, evening and week-end playground activities in the store parking lots, a community center, and a job-training program that has brought hundreds of Sears' neighbors on the payroll.

It seems surprising, at first glance, that some cities experience riots. For example, New Haven suffered considerable violence in 1967 despite the fact that it has the highest per capita urban-renewal allocations in the country — $930 per person. Yet, only 17 per cent of the 5,291 new housing units built and planned in the city were for low-income families. During the 1950's, New Haven's urban renewal was directed to construction of traffic routes and highways at the expense of ghetto dwellers. Another source of unrest was the city's program of *scattered-site public housing*. This plan, designed to break up concentrations of ethnic and income groups, was seen by many black people as an attempt to dissipate their political power and destroy their neighborhoods and group effectiveness.

Note also the difference between the threat of violence and actual disorder. A civil-rights group generated considerable publicity against one nationally known company for its alleged unfair employment practices, but when riot occurred in the company's home city the company escaped unscathed although considerable damage occurred near it to property of others. Why? The threats were for publicity. The rioters knew about the company's long-standing support of community activities and espousal of black-operated businesses.

Black people themselves may be the major victims of riots. In a 1967 survey, 65 per cent of the Negroes questioned said they felt unsafe on the streets, compared to 51 per cent of the whites who expressed such a concern.

The worst of the civil disorders may have passed, but odds are that scattered incidents will continue because many of the factors which lead to riots persist. Although you can make approximate predictions about who may become victims of violence, you can never know for sure because irrational events frequently occur under conditions of extreme emotional stress.

In short, you and your business may become a victim of civil unrest. You should be prepared for such a possibility, no matter how remote you consider it. The next chapter contains suggestions for preparing against riot.

If
Riot
Strikes...

Does the business community have a major responsibility to help cope with urban disorders?

"Yes," say companies by more than a three-to-one majority in replying to a National Industrial Conference Board survey of 356 American companies. The responsibility, as they see it, is to prevent disorders by removing the cause – a poor economic and social environment. Yet riots may break out despite the best efforts to improve the environment or before those efforts have taken effect. What then?

Once a riot occurs, the companies surveyed see the corporate role as one of protecting employees and property and maintaining the company's public services. They also advise supporting local authorities.

Although many companies have detailed plans for action in the event of civil disorder, the majority of firms probably have no plans worth mentioning. The board survey, for example, found that 75 had such plans but that 126 did not.

What Some Companies Do

Here's a brief sampling of steps a few companies have taken in case of civil disorder:

• Commercial Shearing and Stamping in Youngstown, Ohio, works with other local industries to develop such riot procedures as adjusting work hours to curfew requirements, and notifying employees.

• J. I. Case Company in Racine, Wisconsin, has had its fire, security, and medical personnel trained to cope with civil disorder.

• A St. Louis bank has reviewed its security program with top officers of the St. Louis police department and with representatives of local hospitals specializing in emergency treatment.

• A railroad's security forces are governed by an "informal but clearly understood policy" that they will protect company property and employees, and customers while on company property, but in so doing "will avoid, to the greatest extent possible, violent acts or acts antagonistic to urban minorities."

• A midwest oil company's plan includes keeping its flammable products, which could increase destructiveness, out of the hands of rioters. Standard Oil of California spells out its procedure more specifically: "Wherever a riotous situation prevails, we take immediate steps to preclude bulk petroleum deliveries from entering the affected area. Further, service stations are closed down where called for."

• Banks in the Philadelphia Clearing House Association have agreed on a broad plan of action. They obtained permission from regulatory authorities to close at the first sign of civil disorder. Branch managers were instructed to place all cash and, depending on available time, important records and expensive equipment in the vault, which was to be immediately closed under time-lock protection. Employees and customers would be urged to stay on the premises until the rioting ceased or until arrangements could be made through the main office for their safe removal under police escort.

Statistics on the Watts riot in Los Angeles testify to the seriousness of the problem. Property damage amounted to $40 million, with 600 buildings destroyed by fire and looting. Local businessmen sustained many of those losses. Experts agree that companies can reduce damage if they have a written emergency procedure and make sure that the key people know their responsibilities.

Corporate Guidelines

Every company's situation and circumstances differ, so each will have to develop its own guidelines for emergency control, but the outline which follows contains suggestions for what all plans should cover.

Introducing the Plan

First, make clear that your proposals cover emergencies generally, not riots only. Define an emergency. It can range from the berserk individual, to the fighting of two or more employees on company property, through the spectrum of unexpected events, including the bomb threat or fire, up to a major riot in an area surrounding company property, with hundreds or more people involved. Emphasize that you may have no warning of the emergency, as with a bomb threat or fire, but that usually, as with a riot, you can count on a little notice.

Next, assign one man the responsibility for directing a plan and name a deputy who takes over in his absence. Often, you should name at least two deputies, clearly defining their order of precedence. The plan should also name and define responsibilities of the key employees for fire protection, safety, first aid, etc.

Finally, list the objectives in the introduction. The first is the personal safety of employees and others who may properly look to you for aid, such as authorized visitors on company property. The second is protection of company property, including the real estate, equipment, raw materials, work in process, and finished products. The third objective is continuance of production or service to the extent feasible.

Preparation of the Company Facilities

The plan should make clear that your basic posture is defensive and preventive, not aggressive. To protect people and property, your program should include provisos such as these:

1. Make your installation as secure against *invasions* as the physical location will permit and as practical considerations

will indicate. In a sensitive urban area, consider using high, chain-link fences, barred or unbreakable glass or high-strength polycarbonate plastic windows, and reinforced doors.

2. Make a decision about a guard force. Consider these questions: Do you need a security force at all? Perhaps you can have adequate protection in off-business hours with electronic and other mechanical devices. If you decide that you need more than mechanical protection, do you want the guards to be your own employees or supplied by a guard service? Do you need the guards during off-business hours only? Or do you need them around the clock? Only you can answer these questions; however, your insurance underwriter and the local police and fire departments can offer good advice.

3. Establish a procedure to deal with bomb threats. Large industrial installations, especially, have experienced them increasingly in recent years. Usually, they are received as anonymous phone calls. Although most prove hoaxes, you can't afford to ignore them. First, give someone, probably the director or deputy for the emergency plan, the responsibility to decide what to do if the threat comes.

   Next, establish a plan of action. It's not practical to give specific suggestions in this book about individual plans because physical facilities and circumstances vary widely. However, start your planning with a visit to the local police. Adapt their suggestions to your situation. Few local police forces have their own bomb-disposal squads, but they all can call on experts nearby, usually the military or some other federal agency. Every plan should include procedures for a fast, unobtrusive search by foremen and other supervisory personnel. Every plan should include steps to minimize publicity about the threat — both to avoid unduly alarming your employees and to avoid encouraging the deranged individual who made it.

4. Strengthen and improve fire prevention and control procedures. For riots, assume the worst — that local public fire-fighting assistance will *not* be available. Accepted, normal

fire-brigade training practices are based on the premise of immediate *first aid* fire fighting to be backed up by the public fire department. So, within practical limits, prepare for in-plant, overall fire-control protection. All sizeable public fire departments offer courses to civilians in fire fighting and prevention. Periodically check out your fire and other control apparatus.

5. Have your company physician or other competent doctor reassess your first aid and life saving procedures from the standpoint of the adequacy and availability of both people and equipment. Consider whether your people have the right kind of training. Decide whether auxiliary medical stations, perhaps portable, may be occasionally required near the reception area or in other critical locations where injuries are most likely to occur. In general, these stations need an oxygen resuscitator; wheel chair; wheeled stretcher; sterile gauze dressings; and emergency drugs.

6. Plan for emergency evacuation. Consider emergency evacuation drills for the same reason that schools hold fire drills. If yours is a multistory operation, you particularly need the drill.

Relationship with the Community

As already noted, evidence in the Newark and Washington riots indicated that some establishments were singled out for severe damage because of the widely held opinion in the community that they had victimized ghetto residents through overcharges, inferior merchandise, and high-handed treatment. Although nothing guarantees that your reputation as a good employer and sincere advocate of civil rights will protect your facilities from riot damage, it's highly advisable that you seek to cultivate an atmosphere of respect and pleasant relations with such community-minded organizations as the Urban League, NAACP, and others. That relationship may hold considerable value to you in a riot.

Establish your lines of communication with the public police and fire departments well before any emergency. This should prove particularly helpful in a riot when harassed police and firemen may not be able to respond to all calls. County and state law-enforcement bodies may become involved in emergency cases, so get in touch with them, too. If you have some dangerous situation at your plant — flammable or explosive materials, for example — let the local police and firemen know about it.

Conduct Before or During an Emergency

Although conduct is mainly important when the emergency is a civil disturbance, it can also be important for other emergencies, notably a storm or even a fire. Your major decision will be whether to close or keep open your operation. Riot rumors often prove false. Storms don't always follow the warnings. The fire may be so quickly controlled that you can soon return to near-normal activities. In general, when in doubt shut down. If you do close temporarily, your evacuation drill will prove invaluable. Lock all confidential files. Remove all personal belongings.

If you have a large facility, you need fast communication channels, such as a public address system. If that's not practical, set up a *pyramid* system whereby the emergency-plan director informs a few people, who inform still more, and so on. Also arrange for (probably by local radio and TV) informing employees in their homes not to report for work. This would have to include standing instructions to employees to tune radios to a particular station in the event of any suspected emergency conditions. Use the pyramid, too, in prolonged situations to inform employees to stay home or to return to work.

Establish in advance a standard operating procedure to retain in your facility a minimum number of plant-protection, maintenance, fire-fighting, and managerial people for the period of the shutdown. Include provision for food, water, medical supplies, and two-way radio sets for emergency communication.

Set up emergency procedures, too, for transporting employees out of the danger area when you shut down. This could include both pooling employees' autos and using company vehicles. Sometimes, however, it may be safer to keep employees in the plant. If possible, confer with local government officials on this.

Alert your customers as early and as accurately as possible about the danger and the decision to shut down temporarily.

If the riot or other emergency develops at some distance from your location and gives no sign of enveloping your area, inform employees coming to and from work to use alternate approaches. Take the same precautions regarding shipment of materials or products to or from the company location.

Another question about conduct before and during an emergency involves firearms and chemical deterrents such as Mace. Strong controversy rages on this subject, but the cons outweigh the pros: Don't allow your guards or other personnel to carry arms or chemical deterrents, with these exceptions:

• When contractual provisions with the Defense Department or other government agencies require company guards to be armed.

• In the relatively rare situation in which the company guard, as a fully deputized police officer, receives on-the-spot orders to use a firearm or deterrent by a government police official who issues the weapon to him.

When guards do employ weapons as outlined in the preceding situations, they should use them only to defend themselves or any other person from assault. At the onset of a riot, for example, guards should be drawn within the perimeters of company property and preferably inside fences or buildings to avoid provocation. The protection of company property lies primarily, if not exclusively, within the domain of public officials. Guards shouldn't use their weapons to protect property — only people.

Communication to Employees

Appraise the extent to which you should communicate about riot planning to employees. Weigh the possibility of unduly alarming some. These guidelines seem appropriate: Communicate about disaster planning generally — fire, explosion, flood, riot, etc. — but not about riots only. Prepare a brochure or other document detailing complete procedures. Give each employee two copies, one for work and one for home. (See sample letter of Appendix 2 for a guide.)

Ignorance of the facts generally proves more disturbing than knowledge of what the facts are. Many companies find themselves especially vulnerable here, lacking a plant newspaper, periodic letter, or even a program for oral employee communication.

Edward J. Kneeland, manager of employee communication for General Electric points out:

> Employee communication is rarely effective if it's sporadic. It must be on a regular basis. Then supplemental communication on special subjects, such as civil disturbance, can win greater attention and significance. A one-shot communication on possible civil disturbance may create a temporary stir, but then it would be quickly filed and half-forgotten.

Regular communication could keep the subject steadily before employees,providing a periodic reminder about the emergency plans outlined in the special brochure or letter.

Although expensive, an emergency communication center may pay for itself many times over during a crisis. The center would control the public-address system, dispensing information that would prevent costly mass hysteria during an emergency. The center could be provided with police-band radios to keep up with the situation outside your facilities and also to communicate with the police, fire, and other appropriate organizations if telephone trunk lines are disrupted outside your building. The inside telephone switchboard should be protected to prevent disruption of internal service, at least. The communication center could also provide a phone number much like "dial the weather" set-ups which would have taped messages during an emergency.

The following are miscellaneous considerations for your emergency plan:

• Can you secure your elevator system — both for freight and passengers — so that you can prevent outsiders from using it? You can install relatively secure master controls.

• Are emergency stairways secure from outside entry?

• Do you identify employees with I.D. cards or other devices? Many companies require identification, at least to enter the building after normal working hours. You can sell the idea to employees on the basis that it protects them and that it may benefit them when they need to identify themselves as your employees.

• Have you made provisions to protect vital records? Loss of papers such as tax reports may prove costly, if not disastrous.

• Have you plans for public relations? Press, radio, and television people may demand information or statements. Give somebody the responsibility for this.

• Do you have a plan for continuing operations should your facilities become inaccessible for longer than one day? This would include provision for setting up skeleton operations at another of your facilities or in rented space, such as a hotel or motel.

One special consideration involves emergency power. If you have it or are considering installing it, you may feel that you have done all that's possible to protect yourself in case of a blackout. Not necessarily true. Emergency equipment may not work effectively if you have approached the problem of a blackout from the wrong direction — from the standpoint of the equipment rather than from the viewpoint of the people who would suffer from a power failure.

Basic sources of emergency power include batteries, generator sets, and alternate utility services. This isn't the place to delve into the technical aspects that help determine which alternative you should pick, but it is the place to pose questions and suggest answers related to the people problems in a possible power failure:

• Will your equipment provide safe exit for employees? Is it sufficient to operate elevators long enough for people to get out? Will it power emergency lights in dark corridors and stairways?

• Will your emergency power system react immediately? Some systems do not, and the powerless state, even if it lasts only a moment or two, may be long enough for panic to develop.

• Will a blackout lead to any safety hazards with your factory equipment? What about cranes, electric furnaces, etc.?

• Can you, and do you, easily and periodically test the emergency equipment? It needs regular checking.

• Have you communicated to employees about your emergency facilities and about what they should do in case of a blackout? It reassures them to know what provisions you have made and what you expect from them.

The Special Emergency

Signs point to the limited-target civil disturbance. The objective may be just one company. Take the case of a sizeable midwestern company, located in the middle of a slum. Of more than 1,500 employees, only a handful were Negroes — all in janitorial service. The company was old, well established, prosperous, and paternal. Its employees averaged an exceptional 12 years of service. Management and nearly all the other employees virtually ignored the immediate neighbors to the plant — until a militant civil-rights group made a series of demands which boiled down to the insistence that the company hire more blacks. At first, management ignored these, too. When employees were molested coming to and from work, windows broken in the plant, and a fire bomb thrown on the roof, management panicked, met with the protestors, and eventually gave in to many of their demands.

If the riot focuses on you, your only recourse is as already prescribed during the disturbance. But you can and should do several things before such an emergency occurs. For example:

1. Don't be afraid to meet with and listen to the group making demands such as those levelled at the midwestern firm.
2. But determine who the group is. For example, how large is its membership? How close is it to community thought-leaders? To what extent is its request similar to those from other groups?
3. Do homework on the grievances cited. Management's most common error today lies in responding out of ignorance about the circumstances behind the complaint. At the start, assume that the grievant has both sincerity and the potential for justice on his side. Change that assumption only if your investigation proves it false.

4. Deal firmly, fairly, and from a position of as much strength as you can muster with the grievant. Don't vacillate. Don't panic.
5. Promise action only if it's warranted by the circumstances, if it seems feasible, and if you are reasonably sure you can accomplish it.
6. Follow up with a report on what you have done.
7. Gauge the extent of your public communication to the volume of press coverage of the dispute, as generated by the complaining group. There will always be some such coverage because the protestor's prime purpose is publicity. The extent of the continuing coverage should determine the degree to which you "go public."
8. If a union represents any of your employees, keep your lines of communication open with its representatives to minimize friction and misunderstanding. Often, the grievance concerns both management and the union.
9. Don't be afraid to turn down the demands, but only if you have a good case for denial. Let the protestor know that you, too, are ready to go to the press with your story — but be sure that you have a credible, positive story to tell.

The midwestern company did not have a good story. It had to agree to employ more black people, to engage in more community activity, to contribute funds to a proposed community recreation center, and to provide extensive training for the hard-core jobless. Although the situation finally calmed down, it cost management heavily in time, effort, money, and reputation — an expense that would have been much lower if the company had bestirred itself much earlier.

Serendipity and Emergency Planning

"I can't say that I have enjoyed the experience," says the midwestern firm's president, "but it hasn't been all bad. It has really shaken us up — especially in our personnel practices. We're doing some things now in employee motivation that have already paid off in higher productivity. Before the civil-rights problems, it would never have occurred to us to even try such things."

Planning for riots or other emergencies may turn up unexpected benefits — serendipity. But relatively few companies ever find the serendipity because they never "get around to" such matters. Consequently, the opposite of serendipity may occur; minor emergencies may snowball into major ones.

Employee morale — especially for women — definitely improves when emergency plans are settled. A plastic maker, who for years had trouble persuading women to work on his second shift, suddenly had several first-shift women volunteer to go on the later, better-paying turn. "Your new emergency plan makes us feel better," they explained. The manufacturer had never anticipated that dividend of the emergency plan.

Emergency planning can even improve a company's reputation for efficiency. A toy manufacturer, which had put up a chain-link fence around its plant in a run-down area, found its sales spurting noticeably in its own neighborhood. The explanation of one customer: "You people are on the ball with that fence and the other things I hear you're doing. I figure maybe you're on the ball with this wagon, too."

The fence led to other, more positive actions. "After we put it up," recalls the personnel manager, "I got to thinking that it wasn't a very positive thing, even though necessary. For the first time, some of us went out into the community and got involved. Our activities there are still quite minor, but we got out of our rut."

Emergency planning can lead to new and promising directions.

19 It's Only the Beginning

New York City lost 17,000 industrial jobs each year in the decade ending in 1967. Nine of ten major American cities have lost manufacturing jobs during the last ten years. That's only one indication of the urban crisis, but it's one that hits business and industry with particular force.

Alfonso Cervantes, mayor of St. Louis, comments:

> The traditional reasons that industry bids good-bye to the city administration and all that it stands for are taxes, congestion, smog, stickups, racial tension, inadequate schools, an unfavorable labor market, unsympathetic labor leaders, and lack of quality manpower. . . . The eroding tax base, the mounting cost of escalating the services required for the disadvantaged, the vicious circle of unemployment in three-generation relief families, the unwillingness of welfare recipients to go off relief and seek a job for fear of not being able to get back on the relief rolls, the islands of poverty amidst the sea of plenty, broken homes, latch-key children, promiscuity, vandalism, irresponsibility, slums created both by absentee landlords and present tenants, glue-sniffing, drugs for kicks, racial hatreds and violence, youth out of school and out of work, refusing to soil their hands for $1.25 an hour — all of these are the growing, growling prelude to social disturbances that could become pressurized and erupt into a massive series of super-Watts in our American cities within the next generation. That is, unless industry galvanizes its vast resources to help.

Yet, business can't do it all. It hasn't the resources, despite its "vastness." General Electric's manager of equal opportunity-minority relations, Frank J. Toner, expresses a concern that many other businessmen have also voiced:

> Although industry is increasingly committing its resources to get at this urban problem, my doubts persist that our efforts, despite their size, will be effective soon enough.

Franklin Lindsay, the president of Itek, has commented on "signs of disillusionment" at some companies. But industry, along with the nation's other institutions, must make a start toward easing the urban crisis.

Walter Lippman says that the central problem facing Americans today is not war.

> The problems that haunt our people and depress them have to do with the grievances of an exploding population living in cities where modern science is producing a revolutionary environment. The general sense of insecurity is a natural aspect of this change in our way of life.

Where Hope Exists

To the extent that economic progress can indicate hope, there's reason for optimism concerning black people, the principal — but not the only — victims of the urban crisis. Although the economic progress of black America remains disturbingly uneven, there is progress. In 1967, the white-family median income stood at $8,318 — half of the nation's white families earning more and half earning less. The following figures show the median income of the country's nonwhite families, mostly Negro, as a percentage of the median for U. S. white families.

Nonwhite Income as % of White Income	
1955	55%
1960	55
1965	55
1966	60
1967	62

Although the recent trend, which government analysts say continues, still leaves a wide gap between white and nonwhite incomes, it's encouraging to note that in some parts of the nation the gap has become relatively narrow. In the North Central U. S., Negro income is 80 per cent of white income. In the West, it is 75 per cent of the white income.

On the other hand, Southern black families earn barely more than half as much as white families earn. Nevertheless, in the South, too, has come relative improvement recently. In 1967 the median income of Southern black families stood at 54 per cent of the median for Southern whites, up from 50 per cent in 1966 and from 49 per cent in 1965.

Further evidence of progress by nonwhite Americans comes in education. From 1967 to 1968, the percentage of young nonwhite men who completed at least four years of high school climbed to

Table 19.1

Comparative Education Levels for Whites and Nonwhites

	Years of school for nonwhites	Years of school for whites
1960	10.8	12.3
1966	12.0	12.5
1968	12.2	12.6

60 per cent from 53 per cent, while the comparable figure for white men has moved to 75 per cent from 73 per cent. As recently as 1960, only 36 per cent of young nonwhite men had at least four years of high school. Table 19.1 shows the median years of school completed by whites and nonwhites from 25 to 29 years of age.

Since 1966, the median for white women has remained at 12.5 years, while the median for nonwhite women has climbed to 12.2 years from 11.9.

The educational progress goes hand-in-hand with a relatively swift improvement in the kind of jobs nonwhites hold. Table 19.2

Table 19.2

Changes in White and Nonwhite Employment

	Nonwhite gains 1960-1967	White gains 1960-1967
Professional	80%	30%
Managerial	17	6
Clerical	77	23
Sales	22	2
Crafts	49	13

shows the rise in white and nonwhite employment from 1960 to 1967 in the more attractive job categories. In fairness, however, note that the nonwhite base in 1960 for the better jobs was so small in comparison with the number of whites in such positions that the percentage gains for Negroes may present a distorted picture. Also note that nonwhite employment in the laborer category of nonfarm jobs fell 7 per cent in the 1960-67 period. White employment in the same category fell only 2 per cent in the same span.

A government study, entitled "Recent Trends in Social and Economic Conditions of Negroes in the United States, " concludes: "Negroes are more likely than ever before to be earning decent incomes, holding good jobs, living in better neighborhoods and completing their education." The study also notes that "not only have Negro achievements reached all-time highs, but the relative gap between whites and Negroes has also diminished."

In other examples of encouraging economic news about the urban crisis, the National Alliance of Businessmen reported that 12,500 private employers had placed 125,000 hard-core unemployed persons in jobs between the spring of 1968 and March, 1969; of those, 85,000 were still on the job in March. The group said that it was confident it would meet its goal of 100,000 jobs by June 30, 1969, ahead of schedule. It has a goal of 500,000 jobs by mid-1971.

Hope exists on fronts less tangible than economics. In a courageous statement, the National Association for the Advancement of Colored People has urged Negro moderates to speak out against excesses by black extremists. "A small minority of black extremists," says an editorial in the NAACP magazine *The Crisis,* "professes disdain for all 'white values' while at the same time invoking and utilizing, as instruments of controversy, the worst practices of the most benighted stratum of white society, to wit, obscene name-calling, threats, intimidation, suppression of opposing views and violence."

It continues: "Negro leaders have traditionally been reluctant to speak out publicly in opposition to other black spokesmen. But the time has come for speaking out loud and clear lest the entire race be branded as hate-mongers, segregationists, advocates of violence, and worse."

The foregoing are a few of the good signs that the black population is moving toward material progress and a new concept of responsibility. More and more black people have "made it" economically and socially.

But others still have not. A case in point: Divorce and desertion – often the forerunners of juvenile delinquency – plague Negro homes. The percentage of nonwhite families headed by a female rose from 23.6 per cent in 1967 to 26.4 per cent in 1968. In the same period, the percentage of white families so constituted has declined to 8.9 from 9.1.

To the minority-group people who have not made it, industry and other national institutions facing the urban crisis must continue to direct their attention.

Guidelines for Action

You first must face the urban crisis in your own plant by making sure that your employment practices conform to standards for equal opportunity.

On a broader basis, the urban crisis has led to a kind of intellectual crisis in the corporate community. Businessmen generally are resolved to help the cities, but uncertain of what role profit-seeking companies should play.

Undoubtedly government continues to have a major part in trying to resolve the urban crisis, but one wonders if federal grants remain the principal answer. Just before President Johnson left office, still another Presidential commission made that type of recommendation for solving domestic difficulties. The National Commission on Urban Problems, headed by former Democratic Senator Paul H. Douglas of Illinois, rejected Republican proposals of industrial tax incentives as "inefficient and ineffective" for meeting the urban crisis. Instead, it called for a new system of massive federal block grants to states and cities. It did not explain how the grants would be more efficient and effective than tax incentives.

As seen from the examples cited thus far in this book, many businessmen have found their roles for facing the urban crisis. Robert Haakenson, associate director of public relations for Smith Kline & French Laboratories in Philadelphia, draws these tentative principles for action, based on his company's experience of more than six years in community involvement:

1. Get involved. The rapid expansion of private-sector participation suggests that this principle is being accepted.
2. Be selective. A company should identify the situation that uniquely fits its capabilities. Dr. Haakenson says:

> Upon further analysis, some one project is going to emerge as offering the best "fit" in terms of kind and size of problem, location, private and public resources available, timing, and so on. The initial endeavor then can lead to extended involvement.

3. Cooperate. Dr. Haakenson comments:

> Even the smallest problem may be too complex for a single company to solve. Resources can be multiplied, risks shared, solutions enhanced when various organizations and individuals are mobilized. For example, company with company, private sector with public sector, profit organization with nonprofit. Or some combination of company, nonprofit organization, labor, church, minority, or government groups. Every Smith Kline & French endeavor . . . involves extensive cooperation. Also, all efforts should coordinate into total community development.

4. Seek a profit. A company should look for opportunities to realize a reasonable profit in combating the urban problem. Some ventures in housing, slum clearance, and employment have already scored successes.
5. Persist. Dr. Haakenson reminds us:

> The urban problem has been decades abuilding. It will not be solved overnight — or without failures and heartache. So management must be prepared to take the disappointments in stride and reassure shareholders, if necessary.... Employees at all levels should be kept informed and invited to volunteer. Many are eager to help in whatever way they can.

Danger — Keep Out

Some companies and businessmen have unwittingly wandered into booby traps as they try to face the urban crisis. Pitfalls abound, but the following six have probably brought more grief than any others.

Tokenism

Ulric Haynes, Jr., a Negro personnel consultant, says:

> I don't want to be hired as the company's specialist in Negro recruitment or as a public relations man to deal with what they delicately call "the community." And I don't want to be hired as an engineer and then find myself assigned as the company's representative to Plans for Progress or some other government program in the equal-opportunities bag.

The minority-group employee shares the same ambitions as the best of his colleagues whose careers are not burdened by ethnic problems. Another facet of the fear of being used as window dressing is the nonwhite's awareness that he may be hired to forestall the hiring of others of his race. Such tokenism has especially vicious ramifications.

A type of publicity to avoid is the big story with picture in the plant newspaper announcing the promotion of Jim Jones, Negro, to chief clerk in the maintenance department. Giving top-level treatment to a low-level position sounds phony — and probably is. In-house publicity about black employees' accomplishments is legitimate when their accomplishments are genuinely newsworthy. Race puffery in the plant press can explode — on you.

Outside Publicity

When in doubt, understate your case in describing an urban project to people outside your company. Of course, you want and are entitled to favorable notice when your project merits it. But so much publicity in this area has backfired that you should be extremely cautious.

The biggest danger from overblown publicity lies in further alienating the minority-group community. Release information based on the reality of the situation. Give credit to any persons or organizations, particularly in the minority-group community, that have assisted with the project.

Now you cannot win public credit as easily as a while ago for new ideas to help solve the urban crisis. Now's more the time for action than publicity. Furthermore, don't expect much credit from many civil-rights groups, even when it's deserved. If the accolades come, fine; but most such organizations are geared to protest, not to praise.

Appeasement

You put even more than your integrity on the line in responding to strident demands from a civil-rights organization. If the solution agreed to turns out to be a short-term appeasement, you have both compromised your honor and put yourself in deeper jeopardy on the civil-rights front.

A retail-store chain agreed to remove from its shelves the products of a national firm being boycotted. The chain's management began to question the wisdom of its action when its customers, many of them Negro, persisted in asking for the products. Inquiries turned up the fact that most of the black customers didn't even know about the boycott, and many still wanted the items, boycott or not. Management had allowed itself to be panicked into an appeasement that did it commercial harm and made it look foolish.

Check out proposed solutions in such situations with third parties, particularly Negroes. Is the solution honorable? Workable? Will it bring long-term benefits to all concerned? If the answer to any of these questions is no, stand firm. Try to keep communicating with the protestors. Present your story. Keep the door open as widely as possible for continuing discussion.

General Electric's vice president, Virgil Day, concedes:

> In many of these militant actions, few in business really know how to react, because it's a whole new ball game. Unlike union confrontations, rules of the game are unclear, and you can't settle matters by signing a contract.

But he warns:

> We will see a growing minority militancy and impatience. There is the danger of unrealistic public expectations being aroused and pressure for any solutions, rather than good ones.

The Unions

With only a few brilliant and heartening exceptions, unions have long thwarted efforts to integrate many work forces. Jack Star, senior editor, wrote in *Look* for November 12, 1968:

> For nearly a century, most unions have forced Negroes in Jim Crow locals, given them dirty jobs or refused to admit them at all. New laws and repeated union promises are not stopping prejudice.

A case in point: Unions publicized the fact that an estimated 8,100 Negroes were enrolled as of June 30, 1968, in government-registered apprenticeship programs for training to become the elite craftsmen among production employees. The number was nearly double the 4,200 enrolled at the end of 1966. Not emphasized was another fact: Despite the welcome increase, Negroes made up only

3.6 per cent of the 225,000 apprentices registered in mid-1968, compared with 2.3 per cent in 1966, although black people make up about 12 per cent of all the production workers in the United States.

To be sure, some employers have connived with union officials to keep segregation. But union intransigence on this subject generally has proved far stronger than management's. In at least one case, a company had to move out of a plant in the South because the union refused to allow any Negroes, except for janitorial service, in the bargaining unit which it represented.

If you are unionized, you must make clear to union officials that you want an integrated work force because you think it's right, because it's the law, and because you can't afford the luxury of overlooking a significant source of labor supply.

Testing

The Office of Federal Contract Compliance and other agencies have issued guidelines for the use of tests in employee selection and promotion practices.

• Don't let the test stand alone. Use the application form, the interview, reference checks, and job-related experience in addition to psychological tests.

• Select standardized tests with care, looking at the amount and kind of evidence that the author and publisher present for a decision of what the test measures and how its norm group scores may be interpreted.

• Perform validation studies in terms of job performance, and try to establish your own range of optimal scores.

• Upgrade the people who administer and interpret the tests. Provide professional training either on or off the job.

• Review your testing program annually, and make adjustments where necessary.

• Establish, above all, a firm written policy to assure maintenance of ethical standards and professional handling of all aspects of the testing program.

Separatism

This is the most subtle trap of all. Does the ghetto industry which you support contribute more to segregating the community than to strengthening it economically? Is your program a *lady bountiful* project or does it help slum residents to help themselves? Does your job training tend to keep Negroes doing janitorial or routine production work, or does it lead to genuine craft positions?

Those questions are easy to pose, often difficult to answer. We need an integrated solution to the nation's racial and other urban problems — advancing both black and white interests. A *solution* which leads to apartheid really solves nothing; it just postpones the day of reckoning.

Rome and the United States

Many commentators contend that the growth of U. S. power and wealth has brought us many of the problems faced by the emerging Roman Empire. *The Decline and Fall of the Roman Empire* by Edward Gibbon, the English historian, remains one of the better-selling books among bureaucrats and scholars in Washington. Stewart Irvin Oost, professor of ancient history at the University of Chicago, points out that the downfall of the Roman Republic, accompanied by the transformation of Rome into an autocratic state shortly before the birth of Christ, and the eventual collapse of the Roman Empire offer "two wonderful possibilities" for the people to form gloomy, often muddled, analogies with current events.

Nevertheless, what occurred in Rome has considerable practical relevance for today. Like the U. S., the Roman Empire had serious problems of poverty, crime, and decay in its cities, and a history of that empire at least provides clues about what *not* to do in the face of urban difficulties.

Frank C. Bourne, Princeton University classicist, says that the Romans "ultimately gave up in despair" over their cities, and most middle- and upper-class citizens fled to the countryside. In the cities, mobs of jobless, uneducated poor lived off government doles. To keep the poor under control, Rome in the fourth century restricted individual movement, an action that furthered economic stagnation.

Are we in danger of going the same route? John D. Harper, president of Alcoa, speaks for most of management when he says:

> Don't wait for someone to invite you [to face the urban crisis]. And please, for the sake of our free enterprise system, don't wait for someone to order you. . . . We're wed to our cities for better or for worse. So let it be for the better.

Appendix 1

A Communication to
Management at Owens-Illinois

Owens-Illinois, Inc., outlines the following steps in *Personnel Newsnotes*, a monthly publication of its Department of Personnel Relations, as a means to win top-to-bottom support for its integration policy.

1. *A firm and unmistakable stand must be taken by the management.* In hiring Negroes in new jobs and upgrading them into new occupations, the intention of the company must be firm and clear.

The company's action is both a requirement of law and a decision of management. It is not something that the employees or the supervisors have the privilege of rejecting. It is not just a propaganda gesture. Every person in the company should realize that this policy of the company is a condition of employment in this company.

Applicants for jobs should understand this condition so that, if it is unacceptable to them, they can go elsewhere.

2. *Explanation of the program should be thorough.* Where Negroes are being introduced into new jobs, every reasonable effort should be made to prepare the present employees for this step. The company policy should be publicized and questions answered in advance so that people will have a chance to adjust to the idea.

Where the problem can be taken in stride, there is no need to make a big stir – all that need be done is tell the people immediately concerned what is going to happen. On the other hand, where a special educational effort is needed, there are various outside sources of help. Speakers representing Owens-Illinois management, community leaders, pamphlets and excellent movies are available.

3. *The first minority workers must be selected carefully.* The first Negroes in new occupations are trailblazers. All eyes are on them. It is helpful toward later steps if they make a good impression. Consequently, it is

241

very important that employment standards not be lowered in bringing in people who will be the center of special attention by their associates.

This calls for extra effort on the part of the personnel department. As a result of discrimination, the Negro population as a whole is short on education and on mechanical and clerical skills. Therefore, it is to be expected that more Negro candidates will have to be screened to find acceptable employees in this group. Experience has shown that if the person hired is capable and is of good personality and character, he or she will quickly earn acceptance within the working group.

Note that this involves an appraisal of the person's attitude as well as abilities. People with a chip on the shoulder should be avoided. Trailblazers in new jobs may be counseled about the importance of the role they are playing, although most of them will be fully aware of this fact without any emphasis from management.

4. *Recruiting of minority workers should be conducted aggressively.* Since special care is needed in the selection of employees from a minority group, it is not sufficient usually to depend on applicants who present themselves at the employment office. Negroes do not often apply for jobs where they have been led to believe they would not be considered. Special sources that may be used are Negro ministers, YMCA's community centers, high schools, and other agencies active in the Negro community life . . . .

A necessary first step in recruiting is the notification in writing to all regular recruitment sources that we solicit referral of qualified Negro applicants. Schools and employment agencies often assume that Negroes and other minorities will not be considered unless specifically told otherwise.

5. *Minority workers should be treated like other people, not as anyone "different."* Supervisors should make a special effort in their day-to-day dealings to treat Negroes exactly like other employees, with no special privileges or requirements. If a person does not measure up to the job, he should be removed promptly. He should be subjected to the same discipline for the infraction of rules as other people. His minority status confers no special job protection. Of course, he should have company protection against threats or insults at work – as would any other employee – but experience has shown that this need almost never arises.

6. *Common facilities should be shared by all employees.*

7. *Company club, service award, and other associated activities should be conducted without regard to race.*

8. *There should be no segregated work areas.* The theory that Negroes want to be "with their own" has been found to be false . . . .

9. *All eligible employees should be notified of or considered for available promotions or vacancies.*

10. *Ask the cooperation of labor unions and other agencies with which you deal. . . .*Sometimes the white leaders of local unions may be lukewarm or even opposed to this [cooperation]; nevertheless, they should be informed about the company's intention and their assistance should be asked. Sometimes the national office of the union will be helpful in these matters since most unions have nondiscrimination clauses in their own constitutions, and the national leadership of most unions is beginning to put more emphasis than in the past on this principle.

Appendix 2

A Letter to Employees
About an Emergency Plan

The following letter may serve as a guide for giving emergency instructions to your employees.

To: All Employees
Subject: Emergency Information
Few people probably give much thought to what they would do in case of emergency. For example, here are questions which may arise, along with their answers:

Fire

Q. What would you do during the day if you suddenly saw smoke billowing from an office or work station on your floor?
A. First, pull the fire alarm, located on every floor in the elevator corridor near the service elevator. Next dial   the emergency number in the building, and report the fire.

Accident or Illness

Q. What would you do if a fellow employee suffered a sudden and obviously severe accident or illness?
A. Dial   for the nurse and doctor. Normally, the patient should not be moved until help arrives. Give emergency first-aid if you are competent.

Demonstration or Riot

Q. What would you do if you looked out the window and saw a belligerent mob milling?
A. Inform your floor captain who has been appointed to give guidance in emergencies so that he can make the necessary report.

244

Storm

Q. What would you do if a violent storm arose just as you were leaving home for work and you wondered if you could get to work?

A. Dial local metropolitan radio for weather reports and transportation information. Get to work as soon as it's reasonably and practically possible. If the emergency is prolonged, you will be notified by telephone about unusual working arrangements.

Theft

Q. What would you do if a woman employee exclaimed as she returned to her desk or work station, "My purse is gone!"?

A. Dial   . Stay on the line in case the operator wants more information or wishes to give instructions.

We all hope that we never have any kind of emergency here, but we know that emergencies do occasionally arise. If one does occur, we can minimize its impact if we know what to do about it. An emergency plan has been developed to provide the procedures to minimize hazards to employees, to protect property, and to run the business in as near-normal a manner as appropriate. That's the reason for this letter.

What's an Emergency?

An emergency can be defined as an event overturning the normal order, such as a blackout, a fire or explosion, serious injury or illness, civil disturbance, atomic attack, or "act of God" (a sudden and violent storm, for example) resulting in a threat to employees' safety or serious loss of property.

How Are We Prepared?

The building is a steel and brick structure that more than meets city fireproofing requirements. Specific employees, throughout the building, have been trained in fire-fighting procedures. In addition to elevator service, the building has a fire stairwell on the west side and a regular stairwell on the east side. In case of power failure, an auxiliary generator in the basement automatically begins operating to generate enough electricity for stairwell lights and emergency lights on all floors. It can also generate sufficient power to lower all elevators in the normal manner and can keep the service elevator running normally.

Emergency food supplies, if ever needed, can be distributed. Mobile emergency first-aid equipment is available. The medical clinic has a nurse in attendance during business hours (Ext._____). The company's medical director has his office in Room _____ (Ext._____). To obtain immediate help after working hours, dial the emergency number (Ext._____). Guards are on duty in the building day and night.

All first- and second-floor doors and windows are being protected to keep any unauthorized person from gaining entrance to the lobby or the floors above.

How Will You Be Kept Informed During Business Hours?

A public address system has been installed on all floors. Over it, we can give information, advice, and directions in case of emergency. The system, too, can be used to quickly dispel rumors which always spring up in emergencies. The system will be operated from an emergency communication center in the building, which also has contacts with local police, fire, transportation, and other emergency-aid sources.

Your manager will be kept informed through the emergency administrator designated for each component. Each emergency administrator is responsible for:

1. Working closely with the emergency staff.
2. Acting as the information source for employees in the component and acting as the communication link with the communication center.
3. Providing on-the-scene leadership and direction for people in your component in case of emergency.

If a component's employees are located on more than one floor, a floor captain has been appointed to act for the emergency administrator to give guidance and direction to fellow employees. They form a link to the communication center. Names and phone extensions of the emergency plan directors, the emergency administrators, and floor captains are attached.

What About Information After Business Hours?

If an emergency occurs after business hours, public announcements will be made over major metropolitan radio stations. Should the emergency be extensive or severe, you will be notified by telephone of any changes in usual working hours through the use of a pyramid telephone call relay procedure. For those in the building after normal hours, the public address system will provide emergency information.

How About the Family?

Of course, you will want to get in touch with your family – and vice versa – if an emergency occurs when you are at work. Telephone lines get jammed in emergencies. Although our telephone facilities are extensive, they, too, can become overloaded, so observe these simple rules in an emergency:

1. Ask your family and other relatives not to call in. Inform them that you will be able to call out more easily than they can call in if the situation warrants concern.
2. Keep your out-going calls brief and as few as possible.
3. Do not endlessly keep trying to call if the lines are busy; this just contributes to the overloading.

In Summary, What Should You Do?

Here's what to do during business hours if an emergency occurs: If the problem is medical, dial _____. If it's fire, pull the fire alarm, then dial _____. For all other emergencies dial _____ immediately. If the emergency is general and affects the building or just a floor, follow the directions of your floor captain on where to go, what to do and when. If the emergency occurs after business hours, make reasonable and practical efforts to get to work the next day unless notified to do otherwise.

How About . . . ?

If you have questions about any phases of the emergency plan not covered here, please ask them of your emergency administrator or floor captain. He will either answer them or find the answer for you.

Although it's unlikely that any major emergency will occur, minor ones can assume exaggerated proportions if we don't prepare for them. Hence, this document. For ready reference, keep one copy at your work and another at home.

Index